The
SHARe-HoUsE
Survival guide

LIZ POOLE & AMANDA McKENZIE

HarperCollins*Publishers*

HarperCollins*Publishers*

First published in Australia in 2000
by HarperCollins*Publishers* Pty Limited
ABN 36 009 913 517
A member of the HarperCollins*Publishers* (Australia) Pty Limited Group
http://www.harpercollins.com.au

HarperCollins*Publishers*
25 Ryde Road, Pymble, Sydney NSW 2073, Australia
31 View Road, Glenfield, Auckland 10, New Zealand
77–85 Fulham Palace Road, London W6 8JB, United Kingdom
Hazelton Lanes, 55 Avenue Road, Suite 2900, Toronto, Ontario, M5R 3L2
and 1995 Markham Road, Scarborough, Ontario M1B 5M8, Canada
10 East 53rd Street, New York NY 10022, USA

The National Library of Australia Cataloguing-in-Publication data:

Poole, Liz.
The share house survival guide.
ISBN 0 7322 6478 2.
1. Roommates. 2. Shared housing.
I. McKenzie, Amanda. II. Title.
646.7

Cover and internal illustrations by Stella Danalis
Design by Katie Mitchell, HarperCollins Design Studio
Typeset by HarperCollins Design in 11/14 Minion
Printed in Australia by Griffin Press on 79gsm Bulky Paperback

7 6 5 4 3 2 1   00 01 02 03

For our families

Thanks to Colette, Jim, Jan and Doug, Sarah, Stephen, Leonie, Pete, Merrin, Marianne, Dave, Karen, Rachael, Roze, Vera, Tash, Martin, Emma, Jacqui, Kylie, Tran, Janine, Angela, Caitlin, Ailsa, Katrina, Jo, Frank, Ruth, Mitch, Lincoln, Anthony, Sana, Annemarie, Kay, Ben, Suzie, Kirsty, Virginia, our housemates Ruth, Sarah and Annie and all the other people we interviewed for this book. Thanks also to Cathy Jenkins at HarperCollins and Cathy Smith our editor, the tenancy advice services around Australia (particularly Lisa Wilkins), community legal centres, Flatfinders, Gayshare, Maxine from Parentlink and all the other agencies who kindly agreed to be interviewed for the book.

CoNTeNTs

ABOUT THIS GUIDE

Sharing a home doesn't have to be a nightmare on your street. The aim of this guide is to help you navigate through the minefield of shared housing. From scanning the newspaper share-accommodation ads on a Saturday morning, to arguing with your housemate on the day you move out over who owned the ice-cube trays, this guide has something for everyone. At last there is somewhere to turn when you ask those burning questions 'Why is it always my turn to do the dishes?', 'How can I avoid house meetings?' and 'How can we pick the best housemate?' The guide also has real-life stories, some of which are too ridiculous to be untrue.

You may have picked up this guide because you have just unrolled the futon in your tenth new share-house this year. Maybe you've lived in share-houses for years, or you're thinking about sharing again. Perhaps you need some ideas to help prevent arguments over the phone bill, or you're experiencing a total meltdown and need some information on your tenancy status. Even if you're a real misanthrope and are just biding your time until you can live by yourself, this guide can help you.

If you have never had a problem sharing a house, either you have lived in one of those rare and lucky circumstances that happen once every fifty years, or it is time to ask yourself why your housemates have bought you this book and underlined the section about *housemates from hell.*

Chapter 1

Prepare to share

nobody prepares you for a share-house.[1] It's kind of like raising children or becoming an international celebrity – it's just assumed you'll know what to do. Your parents may not have had much experience of sharing. There's virtually no research into the psyches of sharers or popular psychology books such as *Seven Habits of Highly Irritating Housemates*, and it's only recently that more movies and TV sitcoms have begun dealing with the topic. In fact there has been a disturbing absence of collected wisdom on the subject. Until now.

Sharing a house is common – almost a million people in

---

[1] A share-house is a home in which two or more unrelated and generally incompatible individuals reside and attempt to create some semblance of order and shared agreement.

Australia share – and yet moving into a share-house is like entering into alien territory. Nothing is as it appears. That laid-back roadie you had a beer with at the house interview turns out to be a clean freak who keeps you awake vacuuming the curtains at 4 a.m. And your best friend from school becomes the Mother Superior when you live together.

Living with unrelated people is quite different from living alone, with a partner or with your family. For example, telling your housemate that he or she watches too much daytime TV, sheds too much hair or has crap taste in music is probably not on. It is a strange combination of the intimate (seeing them walk past naked while you are eating your Weet-Bix) and the business-like (giving your housemate the bill for fifty phone calls to Finland).

The share-house has come a long way from its hippy communal-living roots. It's no longer seen as an 'alternative lifestyle' and these days it seems strange to think that mixed-gender households were once considered risqué. Fewer people are marrying and living happily ever after, and many people return to or begin sharing after the break up of a relationship. Even Princess Diana 'flatted' before she hooked up with the royal family (maybe she should have stayed in her share-house).

THE GOOD, THE BAD AND THE UGLY OF SHARING

There are many positives about sharing, but also many pitfalls. The future's never certain in the land of shared accommodation. You can move in and out relatively easily, but then again so can your housemate. Everything will be going along peacefully, then one day you'll wake up in a war zone – someone's set fire to the kitchen or done a runner with the kitty money, all because the milk was left out of the fridge. Similarly, share-houses don't come with established expectations about how people should interact. Do you tell your housemates if you are not coming home one night? If your housemate has friends over, should you stay out of the room or sit down and join them?

A definite bonus is the friends you can make through sharing a house. While you may know next to nothing about each other when you first arrive, by the end of it you'll have more dirt on each other than you do on your ex-partners. Research shows that most housemates share for the company it provides, not just because it makes living cheaper.

But then there's the bad news. The design of most houses and flats makes sharing difficult. The majority of places cater for Mum and Dad and the 2.4 kids. Having one housemate luxuriating in the master bedroom while another crams their air mattress into a bedroom the size of a cupboard doesn't help to foster a sense of equality. Neither is it ideal to share a bathroom with a relative stranger and have only one private space to retreat to (your bedroom).

Making things more difficult is the current residential tenancy legislation. Even if housemates have no commitment to each other, they are usually bound together by some sort of tenancy agreement. In most states and territories the legislation that regulates tenancies doesn't fully account for the fact that people share, and is often complicated and messy. This means that it can be hard to tell who has the right to control what happens in the house and who can kick another housemate out, and there are not many legal avenues to help resolve disputes between housemates.

To live in share-houses, you have to develop survival skills. The ability to do Irish dancing and consume four family-sized pizzas in one hour won't save you. What you really need to survive sharing is tact, some negotiation skills and the ability to tolerate the hygienically challenged. You must be psychologically prepared to embrace share-house reality.

SHARE-HOUSES: BEYOND YOUR BACKYARD

➪ In 1999 the Australian Bureau of Statistics estimated that 900,400 people were living in 'group households'.

➪ While most sharers are aged between fifteen and thirty-four, 27% are over thirty-five.

➪ More men than women share houses (57% of sharers are male).

➪ In Arizona, USA, it is illegal to have six or more women sharing a house.

➪ The majority of share-households (75%) in Australia are two-person households.

➪ Most are 'housemates' rather than 'flatmates' – only around 26% of sharers live in flats or apartments, and over two-thirds are renting rather than sharing homes that they own.

➪ Communes didn't die in the 1970s (they are now often called 'intentional communities').

➪ Over a quarter of sharers were born overseas, primarily in the UK, Ireland or New Zealand, with significant numbers from China and Malaysia.

SHARE-HOUSE REALITY

The first thing you need to relinquish when you move into a share-house is control. This is because your place will never resemble the pristine and funky set of *Friends*. Living at your place is probably closer to the experience of the sane one in *Single White Female* and over time will look more and more like the set of *The Young Ones*. The sooner you accept this reality, the less energy you will waste trying to make it into the paradise it will never be.

Prepare to be exposed. You can no longer hide your collection of Hanson CDs, the fact that you have no friends or that you sleep with your teddy bear.

Learn to embrace pettiness. Living in a share-house, your mind will be preoccupied with trying to solve earth-shatteringly vital questions like 'Why don't I ever get to sit in the best armchair?' and 'How can I get my housemate to change the toilet roll?' Accept that you will get irritated, that this is normal, and that by getting more irritated, you will only irritate yourself. Understand that those leftovers you have your eye on will get eaten by somebody else; that everyone is thoughtless now and then; that sharing a house can reveal more about someone than you ever really wanted to know; that life is short; and that unconstructive whingeing about your housemate can be good for you.

Don't be surprised when you find your kitchen taken over by your housemate's alien abductee support group; when your housemate wakes you at 6 a.m. singing 'I Will Survive', try relaxation techniques. Expect bizarre, horrific and humorous things to happen in share-houses. Deaths and drug busts are not all that common, but frightening hygiene habits, secret hurts and petty hatreds are quite widespread. Worlds collide, personalities clash and deep psychological problems are revealed. This is share-house reality.

SHARE-HOUSE REALITY CHECK

⇨ You are not always right.

⇨ TV is the glue that keeps many share-houses together.

⇨ You will probably fall in love with or be the object of desire of at least one housemate.

⇨ Housemates' personalities are fixed for life and you cannot change them.

⇨ Built-up resentments go with the territory.

⇨ This could be the beginning of a beautiful friendship.

⇨ Hell is other housemates.

⇨ Share houses, like milk, have their use-by dates.

⇨ You don't know someone until you've shared a toilet with them.

⇨ Ex-housemates never truly disappear – you'll meet again, don't know where, don't know when.

⇨ It is better to have shared and lost, than never to have shared at all.

Chapter 2

Household legends

You may think that the typical share-house has an overgrown garden, dishes piled up in the sink, a housemate passed out on the doormat and the smell of dope and burnt toast wafting down the hall twenty-four hours a day. While your house may fit this picture, there is in fact a whole range of stereotypes in share-house folklore. This chapter reveals the activities and strange customs of the legendary share-households.

STUDENT HOUSE

Everyone's over-excited in the student household. They've escaped Mum and Dad's and their house is the antithesis of everything their parents stood for – there's no order, no rules and no clean undies. The house is overflowing with bikes, sleeping bodies, op-shop furniture and home-brand party pies.

The household operates in cyclical phases. Two days before the end of the semester, there's a constant blue glow coming from the windows as everyone frantically word processes last-minute essays. The rest of the year they're all out occupying the university administration building, attending Young Liberals meetings or campaigning on campus for More Beer. Most do telemarketing or exotic dancing to pay off upfront fees or to supplement their extravagant Austudy incomes. Typical activities include pub crawls, graffiti runs, serious discourse about post-Foucaultian subjectivities and venting scorn on people in other courses ('bloody med/arts/law/engineering students').

THE PROFESSIONALS

The professionals don't have share-house dramas – they're not sharing a house, that's for the alternative types. No, their apartment or warehouse is not a home, it's an expression of good taste and appreciation of Quality. They just happen to be living with their friends Emma the doctor and Jeremy the lawyer in this really gorgeous house that always has bottles of wine and Stoli in the fridge. No one would dream of eating anything that contained sun-dried tomatoes – *so 1990s*. In fact, the professionals may not even have a kitchen, just a microwave. Often they don't have a house phone either (everyone has their own mobile), and there are no arguments about cleaning – they simply hire a cleaner to do their dirty work. Typical activities include drinking home-made macchiatos and raving about how stressed they are, the economy, and how hard it is to get good help these days.

Interviews are taken very seriously, like job interviews. The hallway is turned into a waiting room for applicants. They take Polaroids and require a c.v. and references. You will be made to feel small and uncouth, unless they ask you to move in.

SUBURBAN HOUSE FROM HELL

While some share-houses are a reflection of style, and others are an expression of philosophy, the suburban house from hell is a practical reality. The occupants may consist of a middle-aged male divorcee, a Christian student, a single parent, their child and a pet dog. You will find the ad for this household in a major metropolitan newspaper, and rarely in a yuppie bookstore. One person may be 'luxuriating' on unemployment benefits, spending their days queuing at Centrelink or attending retraining courses titled 'Climbing the Corporate Ladder while Working for the Dole'. The occupants of this household cook chops, grow their own dope, have their own separate shelves in the fridge (even the dog) and couldn't care less about the fashionableness of sun-dried tomatoes. Compared to inner-city types, the occupants have the privilege of a driveway, but this can be a site of conflict, with the last one home parking the others in.

I made a date to go round and meet the flatmates in this house in Parramatta. They sat me down and fed me cask wine until I was really drunk and agreed to move in the next day, which was their ploy. There was Bob, an unstable ex-Christian ex-bikie alcoholic with bad teeth who was prone to depression, and Suzie, an unstable ex-navy officer from Tassie who was unemployed and stayed home all day watching the

INNER-CITY FUNKSTERS

No chunky pine furniture here, unless its part of an art
installation titled 'untitled suburban artefacts'. The members
of this (ware)house fantasise that someone is filming their
lives. Putting out the bin is a piece of performance art, and a
trip to the laundromat is not some boring weekly activity but
a journey into the amusing and often surreal modern
cultural landscape. Your ironic faux-fur jumpsuit, progressive
techno, designer drugs and first screenplay are the topics at
house interviews. Style is everything and home is a creative
space where you make sculptures out of bar codes and
lawnmower parts.

LOUNGE-ROOM LEGENDS

These houses consist mainly of blokes who dropped out of uni. Their main activity is doing nothing. Secondary activities are going to the 7–Eleven, pulling cones and spouting off half-baked theories based on what they learnt from the two philosophy lectures they went to in first year. The lounge room is stacked with amplifiers and slurpee pyramids. They usually know the guitar chords A, D and G, which is enough to make them believe they are brilliant musicians who will soon be discovered.

LIVING IN LESBOS

As the old Greek saying goes, 'Lesbians are everywhere.' Those nice girls next door may seem harmless enough, but inside they are watching *Xena* and getting a few too many ideas. Maybe it's the way they cut their hair, or the way they only come out after dark and show no reflection when they walk past a mirror. There's at least one copy of Carol King's *Tapestry*, or CDs by Ani DiFranco or k.d. One housemate is an ex-girlfriend of another housemate's girlfriend.

This is the share-house most able to change washers and use power drills. Typical activities include engaging in forbidden passions (secrets that cannot be divulged here) and playing softball. Some are separatist womyn's households – only dads and brothers may cross the threshold – while others are organic and have a well-kept vegie patch, a rosemary bush and a few sculptures made out of rusty metal. Sea-sponge tampons are bought in bulk from food co-ops, and there's lots of guitar strumming and bongo playing.

BEER, BOURBON AND BONGS

You can spot this household by the inflatable beer can in the window and the damp mouldy smell from spilled bong-water. The hallway serves as a cricket pitch, the lounge room as a basketball court. Most of the furniture is constructed from milk crates (a surprisingly versatile household item) and the rest has been supplied by Mum.

Most share-house activities take the form of competition – who can collect the most street signs, who can bring home the most women, who can watch the most sport on TV, who can piss in the toilet bowl from the greatest distance, and so on. The share-house is an ideal place to set the wild man free. They are 'the men who run with the supermarket trolleys' and who play nude football in the street at 3 a.m. Grot is their mark of manhood and they relish the tales of hygiene crimes, drinking binges and getting busted by the cops. Of course, the reality is that the most daring thing they do is not clean the toilet.

Men behaving badly

We had an indoor toilet that got blocked up. So we just closed the door and started using the outdoor toilet. One night at about 3 a.m. we were all out together and we walked past a record shop and there was this pile of Beat magazines. When you're that age you just think, 'If it's not nailed down we'd better take it home and put it in the house,' you know, like road signs and that. When we ran out of toilet paper we put the pile of mags in our toilet. You could read the paper, then scrunch it up and use it. It was really quite rough. The news print was really black, so we probably all had black arses. About three months later it was getting towards winter and we decided to open up the indoor toilet door again. It was so clean, the bacteria had completely eaten away everything, totally unblocked it.

— Matt

The first house I lived in was when I was eighteen. I was very a young country girl and I didn't know anyone who had lived in a share-house, I just knew you got the Saturday Age. So I go round to this run-down weatherboard house in Airport West. There were three guys living there and they wanted an impressionable young thing like me to do all the cooking and cleaning. They were all engineers and union organisers. So it was a really blokey house, pizza boxes everywhere. When we wanted to do the dishes, the plates would just be left in the backyard till it rained. Then they would be brought back in again and just wiped down and that would be it. Not long after I moved in someone punched a hole in the kitchen wall, so they could pass beers to the back garden rather than walk through the back door.

The guys had very different personalities. One of them was a football player whose mother still did his washing, even though he was thirty. She put surprises in his washing, like bags of lollies, when she sent the washing back. She bought his clothes for him, even though he was earning $70,000 a year.

— Catherine

GIRLS BEHAVING BADLY

Men are secretly scared of all-women households because these are places where women rule. They Napisan their whites, change their own light bulbs, kill their own spiders and have a nude 'gods of football' poster pinned to the toilet door. The phrases 'must have a life' and 'house-trained' will feature highly in the house ad. At the interview they will be interested in your white goods and how sociable you are, and will offer you a range of herbal teas.

The house has a glass ceiling and is a Bermuda triangle for moisturisers. Menstrual cycles may synchronise, but there can be serious personality clashes: heal-your-life personal development devotees versus football fanatics, or DIY liberal feminists debating those of the non-essentialist post-modern persuasion. The occupants of this house are proud of the fact that while guys may come and go, the toilet seat is always down.

FERAL HOUSE

You can smell a feral house from the street – that heavy aroma of Chai, natural body odours and essential oils. Doors and windows are rarely locked (there is nothing worth stealing except drugs) so anyone can wander in. The population in the feral house fluctuates widely, as people string up hammocks in the hallway or park their bus out in the street to create an extra bedroom. The level of organisation in a feral house also varies, from free-range to highly complex communal rosters. The occupants share not just the house, but a philosophy, and have a common goal to reduce, re-use and recycle. There can be major power struggles over who has the most authentic lifestyle, vegetarianism versus veganism, what's natural and what's not.

TVs and electrical appliances may be forbidden, and everything must be made out of woven materials, wood or clay (unless it's a house of cyber-feral techno crusties). Sleeping in the front bedroom is not recommended – it can be noisy with all the kombis chugging past and the protest-techno pumping out of the peace bus in the street. Some housemates don't worry about cleaning – Magic Happens! The dishes are present in the moment allowing the wisdom to emerge. Wind can be a problem, as can the neighbours complaining about pre-modern pagan rituals such as naked sun worshipping and fire-stick twirling.

Postcard from Byron

The first house I lived in was a hippy house in Byron Bay. Things are so different up there, it's a different culture. We didn't really lock the doors – some of them didn't even have locks. People just used to come and stay and eat our food and use our hot water. If you tried to complain or to assert yourself, it just wasn't cool. If you tried to be organised or anything you were seen as being too uptight.

One time this guy who was driving through Byron stayed for a night. He had this girl with him. No one knew who she was, but she decided to move in. No one asked her, she just set up her bedroom in a corner of the lounge. She put down her mattress and her stuff. Then she asked me if she could have a potato. I gave her one, and she sat facing the wall, peeling it. Somehow she made it into this bong kind of thing, and just sat there facing the wall, smoking it. She put her own pictures up in her corner of the lounge, like it was her bedroom. She'd just sit on her mattress with the potato. No one really spoke to her.

– Mahalia

. . . AND OTHERS

Goths

In the gothic scene there is a hierarchy – the most important goths are really worshipped. I lived with some of them in Canberra. One guy had sharpened his canine teeth into fangs. There was only one club that they'd go to. The goths really believed that the sun would affect them, so they wouldn't go out of the house until dark. All the windows in the house were blacked out. The only light was from candles, and everyone sat around watching a Sisters of Mercy video twenty-four hours a day.

– Michael

We're here, we're queer

In my last house, we were all gay. There was always someone different at breakfast. We used to have bonking competitions to see who could make the most noise. We never cooked in the house – the fridge was full of drugs, but it was always clean. I got sick of living just with men. If you are having a relationship with a person of the same sex you want to know the other side, you want to live with people of the other gender.

– Ashley

Chapter 3

Better homes
and gardens

how do you set the stage for successful share-house living? The kind of experience you have living in a share-house does not just depend on whether you are living with a control freak or a slob. The design of the house can have a big impact on the dynamics. This chapter provides tips on finding and landing your share-house and helps you consider whether to establish your own house or move into one that has already been established.

HOUSE DESIGN

The ideal share-house should provide enough private space for you to get away from your housemates, as well as having communal spaces where you can interact. But most houses are not designed to be share-houses, so you'll be required to be creative. Some poor but ingenious households have created bedrooms out of backyard sheds, laundries and verandahs. Many use curtains for bedroom doors and old office partitions for walls.

Once I went for a house interview, and this guy who was showing me around opened up the cupboard under the stairs and said, 'This is my room,' and there was a li-lo and all his clothes. He paid less rent. The room that was vacant was actually a laundry out the back. It still had the washing machine in it.

— Tina

SHARE-HOUSE DESIGN CHECK LIST

▷ **Living areas**: Two separate living areas can be the key to successful sharing. Don't foolishly count your backyard as a living area though. Spending your home life in the backyard is potentially a wet and windswept experience.

▷ **Study area**: It is extremely difficult to get high distinctions when you have to study in the communal area of a share-house. Does your desk fit in the bedroom or can you find a private space you can turn into a study?

▷ **Security**: Check out the existence and quality of the locks on windows and doors.

▷ **Storage space**: Are there ugly built-in robes or old horse stables? These can become a luxury in terms of storage space.

⇨ **Bathroom**: Ideally this would be separate from the toilet.

⇨ **Bedroom privacy and space**: Your bedroom is your refuge in a share-house. If the house doesn't have two living areas, make sure you have enough space in your bedroom to relax, and that it is relatively soundproof. It's a nightmare having to tiptoe around if there are only paper-thin walls or curtain dividers between bedrooms.

⇨ **Living in a warehouse**: In terms of the flexibility of interior layout, warehouses have advantages over ordinary houses or flats. You can often change features, put in partitions and set up bedrooms wherever you like. But there are legal issues you should be aware of (see *Warehouses: vogue living*, p. 27).

I was a bit scared about moving in because at the interview they said to me 'warehouse dynamics are different'. It's a different vision of space. It has a lot of freedom and creativity – when was the last time you rode your bike or played skippy in your house? We built another bedroom and got someone else to move in, so the rent has gone down a bit. In winter, people walk around dressed for outside, because it's as cold as outside. Because of the high ceilings you can't heat the place. It's like a family here. We've all got design or music in common, and everyone shares the goal of doing the place up. Two of us are gay, the other two are straight and there is one lesbian, so there's a good mix. I've always lived with lesbians because they usually have good tool boxes. If a fuse blows or a washer goes they can always fix it.

– Todd

There are two ways of entering into a shared abode. One is to move into an already established house and the other is to establish your own house. Each situation has benefits and drawbacks.

MOVING INTO AN ESTABLISHED SHARE-HOUSE

It's easier to move into an established rental share-house, because all the early work, like sucking up to real estate agents and the like, has already been done. In many cases, the longer established the house, the cheaper the rent compared to current market prices. This is probably why some share-houses, particularly decent ones, have an evolving lease that changes one name at a time, year after year. On the downside, moving into an established house means having to fit in with house arrangements and rules that other people have set up, at least to some extent. Also, when you are the last one to move in, you are guaranteed the smallest, darkest, weirdest-smelling bedroom.

You can find share accommodation ads in the following places:

➪ in the real estate section of major metropolitan newspapers (and some regional newspapers)

➪ in the windows of inner-city trendy bookshops and cafes

➪ on university or TAFE student-housing services and noticeboards

➪ in specialised newspapers and magazines, such as the gay and lesbian press

➪ on the internet, through chat groups, web sites, emails (currently limited)

⇨ through word of mouth – asking around through friends or at work.

Alternatively, you might like to contact a professional share-house service. For a fee, they will match you to a share-house fitting your requirements. Share-house placement services can be found on the internet or near share-accommodation ads in newspapers. In some states there are specific share services for single parents, the gay and lesbian community and sharers who are older than thirty-something. Intergenerational share agencies match older people with younger people – free accommodation is provided by the older person in exchange for practical help.

ESTABLISHING YOUR OWN SHARE-HOUSE

The advantage of setting up your own house is that you have more control over early decisions about the house. However, setting up a rental house can be more expensive than moving into an established one, because the rent will be at the current market price and you'll probably have to pay connection fees for the phone and other services. If you don't have housemates to fill all of the rooms, calculate how long you can afford to keep covering the rent while looking for another housemate to move in. If you want to avoid some of the costs of paying rent while you find someone to move in, find the person first, then find the house together.

If you are on a low income, you may be eligible for rent assistance. Contact Centrelink for more information. You may also be able to apply for a bond loan from the government department of housing in your state or territory.

The other drawback of finding your own place is that it requires a lot of running around and ringing real estate agents while attempting to impersonate a white professional on an income of $60,000 a year, with no pets, no bad habits and a personal reference from the Queen.

FINDING AND LANDING THE RENTAL HOUSE OF YOUR DREAMS

You can locate rental properties through the 'To Let' section in the property or real estate sections of major metropolitan newspapers (and some regional newspapers). Many private landlords and real estate agents advertise here. Most real estate agents also have rental properties listed at their offices. In some states, private companies list rental properties and you can pay a fee to view properties from their listings.

ESSENTIAL EQUIPMENT FOR LIVING IN RENTAL HOUSES

➪ A level, so that you don't sleep with the blood rushing to your head

➪ Raincoat

➪ Back door

➪ Machete for hacking your way through backyard jungle

➪ First-aid kit for electrocutions, rat bites and injuries from falling down holes in the floor

➪ Old couch for front porch

➪ Carrots to feed possums in roof

➪ Air freshener for cat-piss smell

⇨ Hippy bedspread to hang on wall over rising damp and seventies wallpaper

⇨ Life insurance

Dealing with real estate agents and landlords

Obtaining a rental property can involve a process of mutual deception. The agent might lie about the condition of the house and the prospective tenants might lie about their employment, their income and their pet ferret. Some tenants even get friends to pretend they are their previous landlords so they have good references. Not that such a sly, clever practice can be recommended here.

When inspecting rental properties, be prepared for a shock. Rental houses are mostly crap. It is highly likely that you will be required to spend weeks and weeks looking at the filthiest hovels, some of which could be involved in studies about rare micro-organisms and festering life forms. As a renter you have to face it that you are lowest on the real estate agent's food chain. But eventually, if you are lucky *and* determined, you will find a house or flat that is not about to collapse and chose to live there.

When landlords or agents look at rental applications, they generally focus on two things: can you afford it and can you look after it.

On applications, the information you are asked to provide may include:

⇨ details of your current and previous rental houses, including amount of rent paid at these addresses and contact details of landlords or agents

⇨ current work contact details and current yearly or weekly income

▷ driver's licence number

▷ number of persons to occupy the premises, including number of children

▷ number of pets

▷ contact details for personal references.

Tips for landing the house

▷ Have your personal, housing and employment details already typed out and photocopied. Photocopy any written references from previous landlords. This will save you time and landlords and agents will be impressed.

▷ Get in early. Often the first tenants to get their applications in will get the house.

▷ If a property listed with an agent becomes available for inspection in a couple of weeks' time, it usually means tenants are still in there. You could put a note in the mailbox of the property, asking if the tenants will ring you and let you view the property. This way you get your application in early. The agent and landlord may be more likely to take you on because they want to get new tenants in without delay.

▷ It can be easier to succeed in getting a house if you are dealing directly with the landlord, rather than the agent. At the inspection, you get to suck up to the landlord directly in person, rather than just in writing through an agent.

▷ If you are on Austudy or on the dole or a pension, pay particular attention to getting good references from previous landlords. You could attach a note with your applications addressing this directly, saying something like 'Although I am currently unemployed, my income is regular and sufficient to cover rent, and as my references will show, I have had no trouble paying rent on time in the past.'

In selecting tenants to live in the property, the agents or landlord will probably contact your previous landlord or agent to find out what kind of tenant you were. Also, they may ring your workplace to verify that you do in fact work there.

Unfortunately, in some states and territories, agents or landlords can ask you for a reservation or an application deposit before you can apply for the house. The idea is that the deposit shows that you are applying 'in good faith' – you are serious about wanting the house. If you don't get offered the house, the deposit must be refunded in full. If you do get the house, the money can be put towards your first lot of rent. But beware: in some states and territories if you are offered the house and don't accept it, the landlord can keep some or all of the deposit! If this happens, contact a tenancy or legal service for advice.

When considering applications, some agents consult tenancy databases run by private companies. These are really dodgy and unregulated, but unfortunately legal. The databases blacklist 'bad tenants', including tenants who have left owing money to landlords. Some of these databases apparently list tenants who have been late in paying rent by as little as two weeks. Some even list tenants who have had the outrageous cheek to assert their legal rights in a dispute with a landlord! If you think your application has been rejected because an agent or landlord has consulted a database on which you are blacklisted, contact your local tenant's advice service. What a shame there's no such database of shonky landlords for tenants to consult.

Discrimination in the rental market is commonplace and although it is unlawful, it can be difficult to prove. Landlords and agents may sometimes be prejudiced but they are rarely stupid, and won't tell you that your application was rejected because you have children, are Aboriginal or gay, for example. If you think an agent or landlord has discriminated against you, contact the Equal Opportunity Commission or anti-discrimination board in your state or territory, and find out about making a complaint.

When you move into your rented premises

Before you move into a rented house you have to pay a bond and a certain amount of rent in advance. The bond is a security deposit that will be refunded when the tenancy ends, provided that all rent has been paid and the house has not been damaged.

You usually sign a tenancy agreement (often referred to as the 'lease') and a condition report (sometimes called an 'inspection sheet'). The condition report details the physical condition of the property when you moved in. Pay careful attention to the condition report. Add anything the landlord or agent has missed. Remember to describe the condition of gardens, fences, outdoor toilets and stoves as well as the usual items like walls and carpets. When you move out the report is used as evidence to help determine whether you are responsible for any damage or cleaning costs. If the landlord or agent believes you are responsible for any damage, they can apply to keep your bond money.

Unfortunately, upholding your responsibilities as a tenant (paying your rent on time, maintaining the property in good order and so on) is no guarantee that you'll never have a dispute with the landlord or agent. While many landlords are reasonable people, keep in mind that their first priority is usually getting value for money from their investment. Some may see your bond money as the means to install new blinds or to have the garden landscaped. Disputes between landlords and tenants are common, and these are covered by residential tenancy legislation. There is a court or tribunal in each state and territory that can hear disputes in a relatively informal way. Tenancy authorities can help negotiate and decide these disputes. It is worth knowing your rights and taking action if you believe you are being treated unfairly.

Of course, there are bad tenants too, who give the rest of us tenants a bad name, but we won't bother you with any of those stories. One of the current affairs shows will fill you in on all that.

WAREHOUSES: VOGUE LIVING

Living in a warehouse may involve signing a commercial lease, rather than a residential tenancy agreement. This has some serious implications that you should investigate first. For example, you may have to pay legal fees and stamp duty for drawing up the commercial lease agreement, and there may be special conditions, such as yearly rent increases. If you have a dispute with the landlord, you may not be covered by residential tenancy legislation, and may have to involve solicitors. Ring your local legal or tenancy service for advice before signing a commercial lease for a warehouse.

BOARDING OR LODGING

'Lodging' means providing a room and may or may not include linen or cleaning. 'Boarding' is when the lodger is provided with meals. Boarding and lodging situations are distinct from share-houses in a number of ways. Decisions about the house are the prerogative of the home-owner and are generally not equally shared. There is a greater emphasis on the convenience factor and the occupants are less likely to have common interests. If you wish to share your own home, you can estimate what to charge a lodger by finding out the rents for rooms in your area. Boarding and lodging are not covered by residential tenancy legislation, so it's particularly important to have clear house agreements (see chapter 9 for more information). A residential tenancy tribunal or similar authority cannot usually resolve disputes in boarding or lodging situations, and your only legal recourse may be through a local or magistrate's court. If you want advice, your state or territory community legal centre, department of fair trading or consumer affairs may be able to help.

SHARED HOME OWNERSHIP

Sometimes, unrelated people may buy a house together and become joint owners. Legally, they are known as tenants-in-common. An advantage of shared ownership is the option to renovate so that you can have your own bathroom, for example. Most people who enter into shared ownership draw up a legal contract about various aspects of the arrangement, such as what proportion of mortgage repayments each owner will make, what rights owners have to rent the property, arrangements for selling a share of the property and financial arrangements regarding repairs, rates, etc.

SQUATTING

Some people set up their share-house by occupying a vacant building. In some cases the neighbours don't even know the house is a squat because the property is so well kept. But squatting is risky. If the owner of the property discovers people living in their house and wants them to leave, the police can potentially charge the occupants with trespassing or with breaking in. There have been cases where the owner has let squatters stay on if they have kept the property in good condition, but these are rare. For more information on squatting, see the squatters handbook on the Sydney Housing Action Collective's web-site http://shac.jumprealestate.com.

Home beautiful

I remember one day my bedroom wall fell down and we just gaffer-taped it back up. It was that kind of house. It was one of those private deals and the landlord would never do anything, the kind of place that backpackers moved into — you wouldn't ask any questions and you wouldn't really know that they were there. There was a huge hole in the bathroom floor. You had to be careful in there if you were drunk. One night one of the backpackers got his leg caught in it.

— Sarah

I lived in this house that used to be a funeral parlour that had thirty-six rooms. About eleven people lived there. The lounge room used to be where they had the service, with arch windows and wood panelling. My bedroom was the little chapel. It was a pretty cold place too. One of our housemates thought he saw the ghost of a little girl squatting in the corner of a room. That house was so creepy, we used to share beds mainly because we were so scared. You'd get up in the morning and you'd find a dead bird in the bath. Or bits of wood would drop off from above the doorways in the night. I used to have this ritual that it was safe to get out of bed after Days of Our Lives started, to avoid the ghosts.

— Frankie

The rents are so expensive in Sydney. In one flat, my friend rented the same bedroom to two people. Louisa went to work during the day and would sleep in the bed at night. Annie would come home from her night duty shifts — she was a nurse — and sleep in the bed during the day. And my friend made a killing on subletting her flat.

– Khai

My first time in the big city I moved into an unfortunate place. It was really cheap — that's why I took it — and I was really desperate. I didn't know anything about tenants' rights in those days. Some very weird people must've lived there before. The lounge had like a burnt ceiling and burn marks on the walls, the owner hadn't even bothered painting over it. One day we looked under the lounge-room carpet and there were all these symbols painted on the floorboards. There were passers-by who would walk past the house and I would get all these arms through my windows. It really freaked me out.

– Erica

Chapter 4

Who's got the power?

there's often an unspoken power struggle going on in a share-house. Sometimes a power difference is a matter of personality, while at other times it is based on the legal status of tenants.

What many people sharing houses don't realise is that they have legal rights and responsibilities in relation to each other, not just in relation to the landlord.

For example, in some houses, the person who sets up the house has more control as the head tenant. They collect the rent from the other housemates, they deal with the landlord, and under certain circumstances they can ask another housemate to leave. In other houses, responsibilities relating to the tenancy are shared, and the legal status of each housemate is equal.

TENANCY STATUS IN SHARE-HOUSES

In a share-house, you may be a co-tenant, head tenant, sub-tenant, lodger or boarder. Determining your legal status is often difficult, and many people only discover their tenancy status and its legal ramifications when a major problem arises. Your legal position will depend on the circumstances of your particular situation.

Whether you are moving into an established share-house or setting up one of your own, it's important to find out your legal position. The following information is intended as a general guide only. Ring the tenancy advice service in your state or territory for further advice.

1. All animals are equal: co-tenancy

Co-tenancy is when the names of all tenants are on the tenancy agreement (or lease). If you want equal legal rights and responsibilities with your other housemates, then a co-tenancy situation is preferable.

Advantages of co-tenancy: You all share the same rights and everyone is jointly responsible. In general, no individual co-tenant has the right to kick another co-tenant out.

Disadvantages: If there is a problem with the tenancy, like unpaid rent or damages, everyone shares liability individually and jointly as a group. Legally, you can't kick someone out. Disputes between co-tenants (for example, over the division of bond, or if someone does a runner without paying the bills) are generally not covered by residential tenancy legislation, so cannot usually be heard by a tenancy tribunal (or similar authority). Dispute resolution services are available in some states and territories and can help you to negotiate disputes. Contact a legal or tenancy advice service in your state or territory to find out what options are available if you have a dispute with a co-tenant.

2. Some animals are more equal than others: sub-letting

This is where the person whose name is on the tenancy agreement rents out the house or a room in the house to another person or people. The person who is on the lease is called the **head tenant**. The person who moves in becomes the **sub-tenant**, and this person pays rent and bond to the head tenant. While the head tenant deals with the landlord of the property, the sub-tenant has no direct relationship with the landlord. The head tenant effectively acts as the landlord to the sub-tenant, and is bound by the same rules that apply to a landlord. Disputes between head tenants and sub-tenants can usually be heard by the tribunal or court that deals with residential tenancy legislation in your state or territory. The head tenant must get the landlord's consent to sub-let (a landlord cannot unreasonably refuse to consent).

Advantages of being a head tenant: If you want more control in the house than other tenants, then being a head tenant may be an option. You deal with the landlord of the property. You can ask a sub-tenant to leave. However, you have to abide by the same rules that cover landlords – this includes the amount of notice you have to give sub-tenants to leave. You also have to provide receipts for any rent or bond they pay to you, and you have to ensure that any necessary repairs are carried out.

Disadvantages: If a sub-tenant has not paid their rent, or has damaged the property, you are legally liable to the landlord or agent for their actions. You would have to take action against the sub-tenant in a tenancy tribunal (or similar authority in your state or territory) to try to recover the money if there is a dispute. A sub-tenant can hold you liable if you have not carried out any of your responsibilities as a head tenant (for example, not ensuring repairs are done).

Advantages of being a sub-tenant: Any disputes you have with the head tenant are covered by residential tenancy legislation (for example, if you disagree over the bond you can apply for the dispute to be heard in the tenancy tribunal or similar authority in your state).

Disadvantages: The head tenant has the power to ask you to leave (with proper written notice); you can't ask the head tenant to leave.

3. And some animals are not equal at all: boarding or lodging

A **lodger** is someone who rents a room in a house where the owner or caretaker has unrestricted access to the premises. A lodger or boarder may not have access to all of the facilities or areas in the house, and the landlord keeps overall control of the running of the house. The house may be one which is owner-occupied (i.e. the lodger lives with and rents from the owner of the house) or a boarding house. Someone may be considered to be a lodger rather than a sub-tenant if they rent a room in a house from a head tenant, where the landlord is not aware that they are there. It is often difficult to determine whether someone is a lodger or a sub-tenant, so get legal advice to clarify your situation.

A **boarder** is a lodger whose landlord provides meals.

Advantages of being a lodger or boarder: You don't have to commit to the legal responsibility of a fixed-term lease, and you are not responsible legally for the actions of the other occupants in the house. When you are a lodger or a boarder, if you want to leave you can move out with relatively little notice.

Disadvantages: Lodgers and boarders have very little protection under the law as their situation is generally not covered by residential tenancies legislation. You do not have equal say in the running of the house, and may not have access to all rooms or areas of the house. You do not necessarily have a say in what happens in your own bedroom (for example, the owner could paint it purple). There can be other disadvantages in terms of privacy, getting repairs done, evictions and rent increases (because you are not covered by residential tenancy laws, legal recourse is not easily accessible). If you are a boarder or lodger, the owner or head tenant is only obliged to give you 'reasonable notice' to leave (what is 'reasonable' depends on the interpretation, and can be very little notice).

Whether you are legally a co-tenant, a head tenant, a sub-tenant or a lodger is often unclear. Whatever you do, seek advice from a tenancy service in your state, and clarify the legal arrangements as much as you can.

No matter what type of tenancy situation you are in, make sure you get receipts. If you pay rent or bond to anyone, whether it is a head tenant or a tenant who is moving out, *get a full receipt.* This can help you to ensure that you can claim your share of the bond back when you leave.

Remember, a bit of caution now can prevent dramas in the future.

I hate real estate agents

This is something I'd never do again. The person before me in this house had been there for ages, and I just took over their room. I just paid that person out the bond, but there was no changeover of names or anything. It became such a nightmare. The real estate agent wanted to withhold the bond, saying that all the rent hadn't been paid. I was expected to be as fully liable as everyone else, even though I'd only been there three months. Now I hate real estate agents. I write down any dealings with them, any call, time of call, name of the person I spoke to. I always make sure a bill is in everyone's name and that you can put names on if people move in. You've got to look after yourself from that legal point of view. But real estate agents will back down if you take them to the tribunal. They'll try to get away with what they can and presume people will say, 'Oh god, there's nothing we can do.'

– Joseph

I hate landlords

I lived in this really crappy house. Even my mum was upset when she came round. We rented it from this bloke who lived in this luxury house in St Kilda. The bathroom had to be illegal – it was just like a few bits of chipboard nailed together. We weren't supposed to have any pets, but there were three of us in the house and we had a cat each. One of my housemates had this dumb three-legged cat called

Goofy, who use to shit everywhere. He particularly favoured the phone, so there were a lot of unanswered calls in that house. One time the landlord came round and we hid the cats as usual. We were standing around talking to the landlord and behind him we see the cats going past the window — we must have left the bedroom window open. Then Goofy wanders in and jumps up on the table right behind the landlord and gets into his briefcase. We could see Goofy positioning himself. It was one of those things that you experience in slow motion — you know there's nothing you can do. The landlord was in a big hurry so he didn't even notice the smell, he just shut his case and drove off in his BMW. God I'd have loved to see the look on his face when he opened it.

— Michaela

HOUSEMATES FROM HELL

A little alarming

Recently, I flatted with a guy who used to wear army greens all the time and had a penchant for military shrapnel art (for example, burst shell casings polished up and turned into vases). In the winter, he used to sleep with a balaclava on, but he found he was overheating so he replaced it by putting a pair of pantyhose over his head instead. As you can imagine, running into him in the corridor at 3 a.m. was a little alarming.

— Genevieve

silverchair's girlfriend

Melanie was a compulsive liar. She pretended she worked on Neighbours as an extra. Every weekday morning, she'd say she was heading off for Channel Ten studios. We started to get suspicious when I saw the dole forms in her room. Then one day her friend rang for her when she was out, and asked me, 'Is Melanie still going out with that guy from silverchair?' If she was, we never saw him; she was at home every night. We worked out that nothing she had told us was true. She said she had done her Master's in Psychology but it turned out to be bullshit. She said she owned the TV and stereo, but then an ex-friend of hers arrived saying she'd stolen them. She said she'd paid her bills too, but she hadn't, and by the time we found that out she'd disappeared.

— Ange

Burgled

We got burgled once. When I came home one night Phuong my flatmate was laughing her head off, even though we had had heaps of our stuff knocked off. I said what's so funny and she said, 'When the cops arrived your bedroom door was open. They looked at your room and there were clothes and shit everywhere and drawers half open and they've gone, "Jesus! They went right through this place."' My flatmates had to say, 'Well actually they only burgled the lounge.'

— Bernard

Naked housemate

Did I tell you about the time I hugged my housemate naked? I was living with my girlfriend, Kelly, and this other woman, Samantha. They both had long red hair. We'd slept in a bit, and Kel got up and was getting dressed for work and I just laid in a bit longer, and I thought I heard her in the bathroom. I got up and I was naked and I walked down the hallway and past the bathroom, and I saw someone bending over in the basin doing something with long red hair. I was still half asleep, so I just walked in behind her and slid my hands around her waist and gave her a hug. And as soon as she turned around, I just went, 'Oh, my god' and it was Samantha looking at me. I just screamed and she screamed too. As soon as I realised, I was out of there so fast. The look on her face — she must have thought I was a pervert. Afterwards she thought it was quite funny. It was too embarrassing. I never said anything to her about it — there was nothing you could say. She'd just look at me and laugh. It's dangerous to walk around naked in a share-house. I didn't do it after that.

— Rick

Narcotics anonymous

It's hard living with a dealer because there's always guys knocking at the door at all hours and constant phone calls, so we ended up just using an answering machine to screen all the calls. There were lots of drugs in the house and everyone was paranoid about security or police raids. One of the guys who lived there was a full-on junkie. He lived in the laundry. We tried to have this house meeting and ask him to leave. He hadn't paid any rent for three months, he was stealing from the kitty and someone had found a needle on the couch. You weren't supposed to use anywhere except your bedroom. We were quite nervous about asking him to go, so we had a few joints beforehand. He denied that he was using of course, did this big sob story, and we just gave in because we were all so stoned by that time anyway. The next day he said he was going to Narcotics Anonymous, but that was bullshit. He really knew how to work people, to use their sensitive points.

— Dean

Chapter 5

The share-house smorgasbord

When you are looking for a house, sometimes you don't have the time or money to be picky – you have to take the first person or first place that comes along. But when you can, it is worth considering carefully who you want to live with. Should you live with a friend, a couple or with someone who has children? What is the ideal number of people for you? What kind of personalities and set-up will suit you? This chapter will help you consider some of the possibilities.

SHARING WITH FRIENDS

The fact that you know more about a friend than you do about a stranger can be an advantage when deciding whether or not to share with them. But try not to let the informality of it all affect your judgement. It can become a quagmire of bitter feuds and broken friendships.

Normally you won't care that your friend spends an hour in the bathroom each morning or doesn't know one end of a vacuum cleaner from another, because you don't have to live with them. But that's just the thing – with housemates you do. Consider this check list in terms of what know about your friend. Refer also to the questions in the interview chapter, which you can adapt when talking to your friend/s about the possibility of sharing together.

PSYCHOANALYSING YOUR FRIEND – CHECK LIST

Major characteristics:	Easy-going or moody
Approach to money:	Stingy, fair or generous
Ability to compromise:	Flexible or bossy
Sticking to agreements:	Reliable or forgetful
Cleanliness:	Total grot-bag or pristine and perfect
Partner:	Sees partner barely at all or joined at the hip
Home or away:	Glued to the couch or out all the time

COUPLES

Couples are people too, but some of them can be a pain to live with. You may find yourself battling the superior power of two, and the dry rooting on the couch when you are trying to concentrate on a wildlife documentary can be really distracting. Consider house numbers and whether there is another housemate with whom you can join forces. Find out from the start whether the couple want a shared house and equal decision-making or if they see you as the boarder. Consider the house. Is there enough space for you and them to have privacy? Or are you going to have to sit in the lounge room and listen to arguments about why he insists on wearing those old purple slacks?

I lived with a couple once. They'd be in the bath making bubbling noises for hours. They were doing regression therapy, some kind of hippy shit, sounded like frogs. It was just awful. The house was really little, so I couldn't get away from them. They were in their honeymoon phase where they'd want to get romantic in the lounge and watch their videos and drink their champagne. I didn't have a desk in my bedroom. I had to study in the lounge and I couldn't concentrate. I had to defer my course for that year.

— Penny

SINGLE PARENTS

For single parents with kids, finding suitable housing can be difficult. There's discrimination from real estate agents and landlords. And lots of people in share-houses don't want to live with children. The high rental costs mean that most single parents usually have to make do with a small flat with no backyard.

That's why sharing with another single parent can be a practical alternative. You can have adult company, help each other with babysitting, and the kids will have a playmate. In some states there are services specifically set up to match single parents together as housemates. One of these services, Parentlink (Melbourne), recommends that you meet with the other parent at least three or four times. You might meet separately first, then have a later meeting with the kids. As well as considering the usual things (smoking, guests staying over, personal interests and so on), make sure you discuss specific parenting issues. Potential questions could include:

⇨ What is your parenting style?

⇨ Do you want an independent or a family lifestyle?

⇨ How do you discipline your child? Is it okay to discipline each other's children?

⇨ What kind of TV shows do you consider appropriate?

⇨ How much babysitting of each other's children would be expected?

⇨ Other issues to discuss include appropriate bedtimes, food and toys for children.

SIZE DOES MATTER

The number of people you live with affects the kind of house-sharing experience you will have. These are some of the differences between small and large households.

Two-person households

Living with one other person can make sharing simpler. If you didn't leave the milk out of the fridge to go off, then it must have been your housemate. But it can also be more intense – there's no one to whinge to about the other one, and it's just you and them, you and them, you and them … When sharing with one other person it is more important to make sure it's a compatible union, as the two-person household can tend to develop couple-like aspects. You'll find yourself ringing to say you won't be home for dinner, having cosy nights in together or maybe you'll just nag and fight about everything.

Three-person households

Popular wisdom idealises the share-house triangle. It's not too quiet, but not too crowded either. It's relatively easy to keep communal tasks organised and under control. But just think for a moment about the famous triangles throughout history – somebody usually got hurt. Take Di, Charles and Camilla for example. The nature of triangles can mean that two-person alliances form. If you are feeling lucky or competitive, maybe it won't be you who loses out. So make sure your housemates are never left in the same room together without you there ...

We kicked Dave out because he was a really bad co-tenant. Dave was a pain in the arse, he was just unbelievable and I suppose we used to bitch about him. He had come from a long history of share-houses, and he had lived on and off with his brothers, so he quickly settled into old habits. There was a catalogue of complaints. He'd piss all over the toilet floor. He cooked for us only once and we all got food poisoning. I think the nature of a three-person household is that you pretty quickly make a two-person alliance, not out of any malice or anything, you just get along with people who are like-minded. The kicking out was just hideous — he got upset. But we sort of thought, well, we are happy here, so he had to go.

– Greta

Four-person households

You have passed the point of worrying about things getting chaotic or disorganised; they usually just *are* with four people. The square means you get to interact with a range of different people and hopefully sample a range of cooking styles. And if you hate being at home alone, you'll probably be happy because there will always be someone else there. But with four people, slackers can more easily conceal their lack of contribution. Don't live in the square if you like control or if you like to cook and clean a lot, because that is what you will probably end up doing, and then you won't like it any more.

Q. HOW MANY SHARE-HOUSE MEMBERS DOES IT TAKE TO CHANGE A LIGHT BULB?

A. None of them, and nobody put the rubbish out either.

Five or more

Sharing with five or more is much the same as sharing with three except there is greater unpredictability, disorganisation and cooking sampling to be had. Sharing with five or six or seven people can turn it into a kind of holiday house – there is plenty of activity, lots of socialising going on, and no one really takes responsibility for cleaning up. Rosters and house meetings are necessary evils and you will probably need to learn to cook cafeteria-style.

I lived in a vegetarian mansion household with seven people, where they had rosters for everything, really regimental. You had to put your name up on the board if you were going to be in that night. They had this big gong and they'd ring it when dinner was ready. You had to cook at least one night a week and dinner had to be ready at 7 p.m. And on the weekend all these people came down and they'd stay in the lounge room. But it wasn't like we had a lounge room, it was called the 'doss room' and there'd always be someone there. Sometimes you'd be cooking for about twelve people on a Saturday night. There was no TV. Some people had them in their rooms, but you wouldn't make it obvious that you had one and you were sneaking off to watch an episode of Beverly Hills 90210 in your bedroom.

— Julie

YOUR PREFERRED SHARE-HOUSE LIFESTYLE

One of the keys to successful sharing is having similar expectations about the purpose of the house. If you just want a place to dump your dirty clothes and store your waterbed, then living with people who expect you to cook gourmet, eat and watch *Buffy* together will not work. Consider your responses to the following questions, and mark where you fall on the scale. The following chart could also be used when meeting potential housemates. Ideally your preferences would be similar to those of the people you live with.

There is a housework roster	1 2 3 4 5	Tasks get done when people feel like it
Housemates cook and eat together	1 2 3 4 5	Housemates shop and cook independently
Housemates get to know each other	1 2 3 4 5	There's no expectation that we socialise
Things are kept clean and tidy	1 2 3 4 5	Household cleanliness is not a big issue
There are regular house meetings	1 2 3 4 5	I'm not into house meetings at all
The home environment s quiet	1 2 3 4 5	It's sociable and everyone's friends visit regularly

HOUSEMATE PERSONALITY

Is there such a thing as an ideal housemate? The ideal will depend on your compatibility, but no matter what kind of person you are, there are two critical attributes to look for in a housemate: consideration and tolerance.

In considering compatibility, think about the qualities you like in friends or in people generally. Are they the same as those you would want in a housemate? For example, do you like people who are quiet or talkative, politically active or artistic? Your housemate's personal tastes and interests will also be important. What kind of TV shows or music should they like? Are they going to decorate the lounge with slasher movie posters or dolphin prints? Are they going to want to talk about cricket or critical theory? Consider also the potential housemate's motivation for sharing. Some research suggests that those who share because they enjoy it make better housemates than those who share purely for financial reasons.

For further analysis of the deeper aspects of your own personality as a housemate, and your potential compatibility with others, please complete the quiz in the next chapter.

You've got a problem

Lisa and I shared a flat in Glebe. She'd always put me down. If I got a haircut she'd say it looked crooked and stuff. She was hygienically hard to live with — she'd leave her toenails lying around and there was always pubic hair and drops on the toilet seat, and I'd have to wipe them off. She never went out — it got to the point where I was sneaking around avoiding her and I didn't want to bring anyone back home. I just had to move out, I had enough. I hate worrying about other people's mess, you know, having to wipe pubes off a toilet seat — it wears you down.

— Kat

Annie and Michelle stayed up at night on the couch eating Crunchies and watching Water Rats *in their floral pyjamas. Michelle had this blue budgie in a cage, right in the middle of the lounge, called Oliver. She'd talk to it every night when she got home, 'Hewwo, Owiver, I wuv you' in this baby voice.*

— Veronica

One morning my girlfriend said she could smell this terrible smell — she says someone's pissed on the floor. Everyone else could smell it, too, but we're all going, 'No, it can't be.

It must be something else.' So anyway, we went to the supermarket and got a steam cleaner and scrubbed the whole carpet. And then about a week later the same thing again. The smell was right near the front door. Another housemate Patrick lived in the front room, so we thought it was probably him. He was going out and getting really wasted and coming home blind drunk. One night I caught him. I actually saw him standing there pissing on the carpet. I said, 'Get out,' and threw him out the front door — he was actually naked when I threw him out, so he slept on the front porch. We couldn't throw him out for good because we were too gutless. So we said look it can't go on, it's the last warning kind of thing, and he said, 'Yeah, I'm really sorry.' So anyway, another week later, he went out drinking again. My housemate John wakes up in the night because he hears a noise. At the end of his bed there is Patrick, unzipped, has it out, about to piss on him. After that we just had to say to him sorry, but you've got to move out. You've got a problem.

— Stuart

I shared with my sister once. It was a disaster to the point where we actually used to hit each other. She'd say something to me and I'd say, 'If you say that again I'll have to hit you.' And of course she'd say it again, so I'd have to hit her because I said I was going to, so we'd have full-on punch-ups. She didn't like my boyfriend, it was a complete disaster. We didn't speak to each other for a whole year after that. With your siblings you don't hold back, you don't have to be polite.

— Kim

Chapter

Discover your inner housemate

Your inner housemate is an aspect of your personality that lurks deep inside your being and only emerges in a house-sharing situation. You may think you are generally a laid-back, relaxed kind of person. But living in a share-house you might discover that your inner housemate is actually a control freak about bills and obsessive compulsive about bathroom hygiene. Or maybe you will find that your inner housemate is a lazy bastard with a deep fear of vacuum cleaners and cleaning liquids. But with time, you will learn to nurture and love that inner housemate.

The inner-housemate quiz

1. **Your housemate has bought a new green-and-gold lounge suite, designed to match the colours of the Aussie cricket team. You really hate it. Do you:**

a   See a colour therapist to overcome your aversion and volunteer to go to the cricket with them next season

b   Try to tolerate it, wait a few weeks, then casually throw your large rug over it

c   Sell it

d   Vomit on it

2. **The thing you hate most about sharing is:**

a   Carelessly folded tea towels

b   Housemates' bad moods

c   Housemates

d   Having to break in because they've changed the locks again

3. **You think no one is home and you are in the kitchen naked, eating the leftovers. Suddenly, your housemate walks into the room. Do you:**

a   Say, 'I'm sorry, I know nudity is not acceptable in the household'

b   Apologise, cover yourself with the cheese grater and rush out

c   Finish eating and leave in your own good time

d   Bend over and start patting the cat

4. You find your housemate sobbing in the kitchen. She says her dog, which keeps you awake all night barking, has been found dead. Do you:

a   Hug her and help her to release her grief

b   Make her a cup of tea and suggest an autopsy

c   Discreetly slip the cyanide bottle into the recycling bin

d   Make yourself a toasted cheese sandwich

5. You come to the last square of toilet paper on the roll, and you know there's no money left in the kitty. You are on your way out. Do you:

a   Leave a note in the house-book that says 'Can we have an urgent house meeting to discuss the toilet paper situation'

b   Buy a roll and take the cost off your next week's kitty money

c   Use your own secret stash of toilet paper

d   Use your housemate's towel

6. For the fourth time this week you are woken by neighing and stamping sounds. At first you think a wild horse has escaped from somewhere and has somehow got into your house. Then you realise it's your housemate and her partner having sex in the next room. Do you:

a   Call a house meeting, at which you will discuss the horror of fornication outside of the union of marriage

b   Yawn a lot the next day and tell her you're a light sleeper, hoping she'll get the hint c   Burst into their room and tell them to shut the fuck up

d   Call the RSPCA

7. **One of your housemates has just died, so you need to find a new one. Do you:**

a   Conduct a series of focus groups with your housemates, to facilitate agreement on the preferred type of person

b   Advertise for someone and hold interviews

c   Move a friend in, telling them the room is more expensive than it is, so you get to keep the extra cash

d   Leave the front door open and wait for someone to wander in

8. **Of the following types of people, with whom would you prefer to spend your time:**

a   Housemates

b   Friends

c   Real estate agents

d   No one

9. **You and your housemate are up late watching *Rage* together. Your housemate has been complaining that they never play enough Savage Garden on *Rage*, and you're sitting there thinking how you really don't have much in common. Next thing you know, your housemate has blurted out that they're in love with you. Do you:**

a   Remind them of the rule that there are to be no love relationships between housemates

b   Explain tactfully but honestly that you like them as a friend but you don't feel that way

c   Seize the opportunity of open communication to tell them you can't stand them

d   This would never happen to you – you watch TV in your bedroom

10. **You hear your housemate screaming, 'There's a naked man in our backyard.' Do you:**

a   Lead your housemates outside as a squad to confront the intruder with kitchen knives

b   Call the police

c   Lean out your bedroom window and fire a couple of warning shots into the air

d   Sneak back in through the front door

11. **Your housemate kept you awake last night playing the banjo in his bedroom. Do you:**

a   Get ready the next night to jam with your nylon string guitar, feeling slightly offended you weren't asked to join in

b   Feel annoyed and resolve to say something if it happens again

c   Dump his stuff on the front porch (after you've had a good look through to see if there is anything you want to take) and get the locks changed

d   Turn up your stereo

12. At the house meetings, you feel:

a   Excited

b   Bored

c   Angry

d   Scared

13. Your housemates often fall silent when you walk into the kitchen and you suspect they are bitching about you behind your back. Do you:

a   Bring in a healer to realign the house harmony

b   Ignore it and try to work out if you are doing something to upset them

c   Sneak around in socks and try to catch them out

d   Think 'here we go again'

14. Your housemate tells you she's really annoyed with you and accuses you of not pulling your weight around the house. Do you:

a   Feel mortified and instantly begin a thirty-hour cleaning frenzy

b   Apologise, even though she gives you the shits

c   Blow up her hair dryer

d   Ignore her and go back to bed

15. A toilet brush is best used:

a   In a rigorous manner, after every motion

b   Once a week or as required

c   By someone other than you

d   When you can't find your hairbrush

Scoring

Add up how many times you circled (a), (b), (c) or (d). The number you scored most of is your inner-housemate personality and is described below. Each inner housemate has a number of rising signs. Refer to chapter 7, Housemates of the zodiac.

Now check your score.

MOSTLY (A) = TOO GOOD

Your inner housemate is pro-active in celebrating the non-violent household. You see conflict as a challenge and are the first to 'raise' it as an 'issue' at house meetings. You want to heal differences and empower your housemates. You love to participate and believe rosters help ensure a creative and caring shared space. You are supported in your efforts by your therapist. Sometimes you feel a little insecure and wonder why your housemates seem oblivious to your acts of Random Kindness and Senseless Beauty. Perhaps they are getting sick of your daily readings from your dream diary. Maybe you have empowered them too much and they are about to kick you out. This could be something to discuss with your therapist.

Type of housemate to suit you: Try and steer your inner housemate towards other enlightened beings, people who will appreciate your positive energies. While you may see those who scored mostly (d) as a challenge, it's probably best to keep away, as your energies will be wasted.

Your rising signs of the zodiac: Clean queen, royal personage, super-housemate, Kramer.

Mostly (b) = Good

Did you lie on the quiz or what? Your inner housemate is perfectly balanced for sharing. In fact, you are the person most likely to have read this book and taken note of all its recommendations. You are balanced, responsible, reasonably clean but never obsessive. You are the grease that keeps the share-house cogs turning. You like living with other people, but you have a life outside of the house. Your housemates neither laugh at you nor fear you, but they possibly take advantage of you. You are co-operative and tolerant, you dislike conflict and you like to be liked. Make sure you don't compromise too much, to the extent that you are not happy.

Type of housemate to suit you: Your housemates probably don't deserve you. Look for people who are tolerant and easy-going, and keep away from anyone who scored mostly *a*, *c* or *d*.

Your rising signs of the zodiac: Super-housemate, royal personage, clean queen.

Mostly (c) = Bad

It's hard living in a share-house, isn't it? I mean, the bloody whingers, the uptight freaks trying to ruin your life. That Mandy really gets up your nose, all that crying and carrying on about one dead dog. And just because some judge said you were vindictive and dangerous, what does that dickhead know? Conflict doesn't bother you, and you can really harbour a grudge. You'll pay bills and do dishes when you are good and ready. You hate sharing and wish you could afford to live on your own.

Type of housemate to suit you: No one.

Your rising signs of the zodiac: Terminator, psycho, recluse.

MOSTLY (D) = UGLY

Hey, you're just laid-back and relaxed – house conflict and cleaning never bother you. You are into avoidance – avoidance of conflict, avoidance of cleaning, avoidance of housemates generally. Your idea of participating in share-house life is flushing the toilet and chucking the rubbish into the neighbours' yard. You occasionally have doubts about how loved you are in the house, like that day they changed the locks on you (what a pack of lovable jokers they are). But let them call you anti-social, let them mock your hygiene standards. So what if you get four wears out of each pair of underpants (frontwards, backwards, inside-out frontwards, inside-out backwards), you're making a big saving on washing powder.

Type of housemate to suit you: Living with other slack-arses is your idea of share-house nirvana. Definitely keep away from people who answered mostly (a).

Your rising signs of the zodiac: House potato, recluse, Kramer.

Chapter 7

Housemates of the zodiac

orget being a Scorpio or a Virgo, when you live in a share-house you've entered another planetary system. The twelve housemate signs and their characteristics have been determined by universal astrological forces beyond our comprehension. This chart will assist you in spotting each sign at interview, appreciating individual traits, identifying negative tendencies and predicting behaviour. Some housemates are born on the cusp of the signs and they tend to shift when the moon is in Uranus.

CLEAN QUEEN

The most mocked of the signs is the clean queen (also known as 'the control freak'). Delicate and highly strung by nature, a housemate under this sign is incompatible with the house potato (also known as 'the slob').

House ad: 'Immaculate house, looking for mature, tidy individual.'

How to spot one at the interview: The clean queen will be wearing white or purple. Interviews will be conducted in an orderly manner, and questions asked from a set list and responses noted. Look for labels and notices around the house. The clean queen is commonly the owner of the house or the head tenant. Will emphasise the importance of cleaning under the toilet rim.

Common activities: Counting teaspoons and labelling potatoes with post-it notes. Often found in the kitchen at midnight checking for streak marks on the washed glasses or with their head in the oven (not trying to kill themselves – trying to get at those hard-to-reach places). The clean queen is known to accuse: 'You've been drinking my cordial – the liquid level is down.' Those on the cusp are too busy writing out rosters to actually do any cleaning themselves – their role is to ensure standards are maintained. They are terrified that you will steal or break something and they are reluctant to share. People born under this sign are partial to symphonies, operas and any music which makes them feel highly disciplined.

My friend moved in with this guy and the very first morning this dweeb comes running into his room, yelling at him that he had used one of his tea bags — he numbered his tea bags. My friend knew that he should move out then and there, but didn't. This guy would check that people weren't using his bowls and plates and accuse people of using them. My friend use to get up really early, use his stuff, wash it and put it away like he'd never used it. He used to pride himself on not getting sprung. This guy had a street map that absolutely had to be in the same place at all times, so my friend would move the map around the lounge room. It would drive the other guy absolutely nuts. My friend lived with him for two years. When my friend left he did a runner — I can't remember why — but in order to sneak out, he had to let down his waterbed by putting the hose out the bedroom window. Once all the water was out, he threw the bed out the window, climbed out the window after it and left. The dweeb had driven him mad, obviously.

—Warren

RECLUSE

The recluse is ruled by the moon and is the most mysterious of all the signs.

House ad: Tiny handwriting that is difficult to read.

How to spot one at the interview: When you ask what they're looking for in a housemate the recluse will say, 'Someone who pays the bills.' The house will appear neglected, and all food is stored in the recluse's bedroom.

Common activities: Not really known, as what recluses do with their time is a mystery. Like most episodes of *The X-Files*, they are unfathomable and often pointless. But the truth is out there – or at least in their bedroom, where they spend most of their time. Bedroom activities may include pottery, listening to Marilyn Manson, training carrier pigeons and writing poetry. It's hard to relax when living with a recluse, as a sudden emergence from the bedroom can scare the hell out of you. You can live with a recluse for three years and still have no idea who they are. You'll even have forgotten their name.

TERMINATOR

The terminator would have to be the least desirable of the zodiac signs.

The house ad: Looks like someone has chewed it up and spat it out – with just the room price and a phone number.

How to spot one at the interview: Terminators will paint themselves as great mates and focus mostly on bills. They will talk about past housemates in a bitterly resentful way.

Common activities: Yelling, throwing tantrums, haggling over money, slamming doors, removing your things from the public area, eating all your food and not paying for it. If you are lucky they may give you the silent treatment. They will accuse you of being petty if you confront them about anything. Nothing ever is their fault. When they are not at home they can usually be found committing road rage. They are often the lease holder (people are too scared to evict them).

If a terminator ever condescends to do something for you, it will be a favour they'll never let you forget. They are blatantly inconsiderate, as if they are daring you to say something. If looks could kill, you'd be dead. One advantage of living with the terminator is that you will probably become very informed about the legal system.

The alpha

My housemate Angus believed that there should be an alpha, a leader, in every home. If he got up at 6 a.m. then we should all be up. He would try to intimidate you, yelling and stuff. You don't live with people like that, or share with them, you live around them. You're always having to think, is this going to upset him? Am I sitting in the wrong chair? He used to blame my dog for everything, like my dog was secretly teaching his dog how to be bad. He treated his girlfriend like shit too. He had no respect for her property. He would break her things and take the attitude that she made him do it. He was really cruisy at the interview. If people are stoned at the interview you should come back another time, when they are not. And you should have a close look at the surroundings. Angus used to punch holes in the wall. Ask them if they have their own chairs or if they must watch their own TV shows — that's a definite sign.

— Daniel

KRAMER

Common rising sign of many housemates.

House ad: Chaotic handwriting with wacky descriptions: 'Fellow alien wanted to share starship *Enterprise*.'

How to spot one at the interview: The Kramer usually arrives late, having been injured last night in a stage-diving accident (no one was there to catch them). Will show lots of enthusiasm, though their questions will seem irrelevant: 'Do you reckon Rubik's cube will get popular again?'

Common activities: Locking themselves out and getting sunburnt from sunbaking nude on the banana lounge. When you come home to discover the back door wide open, the heaters on full blast, and a note that says, 'Whoops, the TV fell out the window,' you know you are living with a Kramer. This person was not designed for the confines of a house. They often run on adrenaline for weeks and then completely collapse. Never bitch to them about your other housemates, because they will invariably repeat it at the next house meeting. They are the housemate most likely to burn the house down.

Nude vacuuming

One night I was woken up by noise at 3 a.m. and found Dave vacuuming nude in the lounge room. At least I think he was vacuuming — the vacuum was on. He's the sort of person who constantly loses his keys, so he'll knock on the door at 4 a.m. or you'll hear him crashing through his bedroom window. We often hear him rehearsing phone

> *conversations in the shower — he'll have this whole fake conversation, he doesn't know we can hear. Once he pissed on my herb plants in the backyard when someone was in the shower. I went out there and saw all the urine running across the concrete from the potplants. I knocked on his door and said, 'Did you just wee on my pot plants?' He said, 'Oh sorry, it's not stupidity, it's ignorance,' and went out and hosed it off.*
>
> — Sarah

ROYAL PERSONAGE

Could you be living with a distant relative of the royal family?

Royal house ad: Designed to reflect their breeding, for example: 'Highly literate, intelligent, into fine wine and creative pursuits.'

How to spot one at the interview: The royal personage won't ask you many questions at the interview, but will smile at you condescendingly and have excellent posture. This is the beginning of you feeling grateful for their attention.

Common activities: Affecting vogue poses on the couch, being on the phone, hating share-house living, moving gracefully about the house, having perfect bedrooms and outlandish hobbies involving medieval costumes and furry animals. They quite enjoy your cooking but feel it would be improved by higher-quality ingredients. They don't know what a toilet brush is, but have been known to use the vacuum cleaner — in their own room. You'll be appointed to clean up the corgi poo.

If confronted, the royal personage will act shocked and wounded, and say, 'Who are you to question me?' or they will mock you: 'God, you are so petty. Get a life.' You'll be made to feel like a minor irritant in their important lives, whining pathetically like a mosquito. Remember, the royal personage should never be touched, and neither should their things.

Living with royals

She didn't like to get her hands dirty. She wouldn't know how to change a light globe, or drive stuff to the dump or carry furniture. She was a dancer. One time she'd been out partying all night with all the other dancers. She got home at about 6 a.m., ate just about the whole week's supply of shopping I'd done the day before and then went to bed and slipped the phone off the hook so it wouldn't wake her. We didn't discover the phone was off the hook until about 11 p.m. the next day. Another time she had been writing an essay and left all these scraps and screwed up balls of paper on the window sill. They'd been there for weeks, so I asked her to move them. She said, 'I'm not removing them, they're art.' I was so shocked, what could I say?

— Amirah

VIRTUAL

This could be one of the best star signs you'll ever live with.

House ad: Words such as 'independent' and 'busy' will feature.

How to spot one at the interview: Will focus on practical issues, and not on getting to know you. Will rush off early to meet their boyfriend/girlfriend.

Common activities: Checking phone messages, leaving and being absent. They may pay bills but their bedroom will be covered in a blanket of dust – their room is really a storage space for the clothes they never wear. You may start to become paranoid that they think you're too boring to hang around with. While this is probably true, their primary excuse is that they spend all their spare time at their partner's place. The house is a fall-back in case they get dumped.

HOUSE POTATO

This is one of the most complained-about zodiac signs. House potato is ruled by Saturn and leaves rings around the bath.

House ad: Will have sauce stains and words like 'laid-back' and 'easy-going'.

How to spot one at the interview: The doona on the couch, Twisties packs on the floor, and the fact that they are wearing pyjamas may give them away. May also appear to be dead or asleep. They will refer to their previous housemates as 'uptight' and say, 'I'm really approachable, if you want me to clean anything, just let me know.'

Common activities: Most often found doing nothing. Other activities include watching Home Shopping or playing PlayStation. Their food and beverage consumption is kind of like Elvis when he was old and decaying. They will get away with what they can, including rampant laziness and noisy bodily emissions. It's always *their* toenails on the couch, urine on the toilet floor and stray underwear hanging on the hat rack. While they are rarely dangerous, they may attack when cornered. The house potato gives new meaning to the word 'relaxed' – in fact they could teach yogis and over-achievers a thing or two. If you end up with a house potato, make sure they keep their bedroom door shut – one waft can kill a housemate at thirty paces.

Chip-packet doona

Dave used to burrow his way into his bed through twin-pack chip packets, pizza crusts, worn underwear and mechanical parts from his old motorbike. The smell was incredible. He didn't use a doona – I suppose the chip packets provided some warmth. One day we counted forty-six twin-pack chip packets in his room. He spent all his time in there, reading or sleeping. You could hear him munching on the chips and he constantly had some talkback radio going. The only time he'd emerge was to go to the toilet, and he always made sure he left his mark there.

– Lee

PSYCHO

Psychos fulfil an important role in the housemates' zodiac, as they alert us to the existence of the dark side.

House ad: Uses a mix OF upPer and LOWer case, OFTEN with a small indecipherable drawing.

How to spot one at the interview: Purportedly very difficult to spot, so go with your gut feeling. They may say they need a shed or basement but won't tell you what for.

Common activities: Being unpredictable, locking their room and having an unnerving stare. You'll hear them shouting at someone on the phone, 'I hope you rot in hell,' then they'll tell you, 'Hey, your mum just rang, she said she'd call back later.' One time they will smile and agree to turn down their stereo at 3 a.m. and say, 'Thanks for raising this issue,' and at other times they will suddenly snap, screaming, 'Stop trying to hurt me, you fucking bastard.' Psychos prefer to smash light bulbs rather than use light switches. Some psycho housemates are just odd, while others can be dangerous. Trouble is, there's no real way of telling, so treat anyone born under this sign with extreme caution.

He seemed nice

I took Sally to the house interview to be my backup, you know, you take a friend along so they can get the vibes as well. Rick seemed friendly and sociable. When we got outside I said to her, 'What did you think of him?' and she said, 'Oh, he seemed nice.' In retrospect she was as mad as a hatter, and I'm taking advice from her. I moved in and he did not move from the lounge room for the entire six months I was there. He didn't see any friends, he didn't do anything. During this time I got to know him a bit better, and he insisted he had been a sniper in a special army regiment like the SAS. He had a collection of books, like Great Machine Guns of the Twentieth Century, Twenty Great Massacres of World War II, a small firearms collection under his bed and heaps of S&M bondage gear hanging

RAVER

This sign is ruled by Jupiter, the planet of disco and pubs.

House ad: Too busy partying to write one.

How to spot one at the interview: At the interview they will probably ask you to repeat things; they are not being rude, it's just that their hearing has been impaired by all the doofing and phat beats. The blinds in their bedroom are always down, there's glow sticks, a floordrobe, a CD player, a mattress and not much else.

Common activities: Usually found sleeping all day or putting the stereo on at 7 a.m. when they get home from a club, rave or pub. Calls are always for them and you'll feel like the secretary taking their messages. They are never home long enough to cause house conflicts, but it is often hard to get bill money out of them as they spend all their money on drugs and the right outfits. They survive on Chupa Chups, bottled water and toast. Their friends can be found passed out in the lounge and their one-night-stands are seen scuttling from the scene by the neighbours. If you want to annoy them, take up vacuuming on Sunday mornings.

SLEAZE

House ad: Will sound like a personal column: 'DTE youthful Ricky Martin look-alike with GSOH and flatette to share.'

How to spot one at the interview: Usually male and wearing their jeans or trousers either too high or too low. If you get to look in their room you may notice the velvet bedhead or special mirrors. They only sit on the couch – never on an individual chair.

Common activities: Walking around in towels and lurking outside bathroom and bedroom doors. Favourite conversational topics include sex, your love life and what you are wearing. They engage in any activity that creates some sort of physical bond between themselves and whoever they fancy in the house (which is usually everyone). For example, they might drink out of the cup you just used. If there is household conflict, they will agree with whoever they think they might have a chance with. They live under the delusion that they are sexy and brilliant, and participate in cleaning activities where they can reveal their allure, such as taking their shirt off to dust the mantlepiece.

SUPER-HOUSEMATE

This is a very rare sign, some would say non-existent.

House ad: Will stand out because it will be creative and positive.

How to spot one at the interview: Unlike normal listeners who nod their heads while thinking of something else, super-housemates reflect carefully on what you say and validate your feelings. They will offer you homemade fruitcake, and because they appear so friendly you will presume they are a version of the psycho.

Common activities: Straining beancurd at 6 a.m., giving, caring and putting the bin out. They communicate well and are unnaturally pleasant to come home to. So why are they living with you? There are disadvantages in living with the super-housemate. They will completely ruin you for living with other housemates (because every other housemate will pale in comparison) and they will expose you as the lazy, thoughtless, pathetic specimen that you are.

SCAM ARTIST

House ad: Rarely seen, as they hardly ever stay in any house long enough to do the ad.

How to spot one at the interview: A scam artist rarely enters a share-house via a house interview process but moves in supposedly temporarily because they are a friend of your housemate and they don't have anywhere to go. If they did happen to attend a house interview, they would rave enthusiastically about your place, ask you a number of personal questions and then go about attempting to impress you. There'll be an odd reason for leaving the last house and they will want to move in straight away. In fact they will have their stuff packed in the car. They can't get on leases because they have been evicted from too many houses.

Common activities: Creating drama, manipulating, telling you their problems, trying to discover your sensitive points, identifying the weakest of the pack, encouraging you to bitch about other housemates (to use against you later), misappropriating the kitty and getting kicked out. Some people can 'work a room', but the scam artist works a whole house. They are more likely than other housemates to have an expensive addiction, which can be a bonus when they score the house some ecstasy. Things will go missing and they will usually win over at least one housemate, who will pay their rent. The scam artist has an air of desperation and the difficulty is that in the early days it is easy to feel sorry for them. But in years to come you will see them again one day, living in another house, watching your TV, with your video, on an island in Spain.

Chapter

Weeding out
the weirdos

Living with other people is a big deal – it can have a major impact on your life. Yet some people put more effort into choosing their socks than choosing a housemate. If you don't ask potential housemates the right questions, and end up moving into the wrong house, then you're headed for disaster. While it's true that you never really know someone until you live with them, approaching the house interview strategically can greatly reduce the likelihood of picking a complete weirdo.

STEP 1 – THE HOUSE ADVERTISEMENT

Approach house advertisements with a skeptical eye. The specifications in house adverts consist of a combination of wishful thinking and discriminatory practice. You've got to read between the lines. For example, the term 'broad-minded' could mean anything from someone who runs a brothel from home to someone who is a die-hard fan of the Bee Gees. For more information about house ads, read chapter 7. For interesting adjectives to use when writing an ad, refer to the list of common adjectives in share-house ads.

Single white female wanted to share gothic-style apartment with gorgeous but gullible female. Looking for someone sane and sensible with flat shoes and their own taste in clothing. Psychos need not apply. $120 p/w each. Available now.
Phone Bridget 04 4129 0876

What a classic catch!
Looking for housemates who are good honest Aussies who prefer Lager Before Washing (LBW). Definitely a non-smoking household – unless photographic evidence reveals otherwise. No vegetarians, but baked-bean eaters welcome.
  The condition of the house will be revealed upon cash payment.
  Rent: $110 p.w.
  Phone: Warne & Co. on 2222 4444

Housemate wanted to share Canberra residence. Magnificent bedroom available in right wing of house (left wing out of bounds). Enjoys power walking, whining and dining and policy making with wealthy friends. Looking for someone who has true family values. Personal references from HRH ER II preferred. No to drugs, republicans, journalists, and no space available for refugees. Rent $4,092 per calendar month plus GST
Call Johnnie on 02 3456 7890 or apply directly to the servants' quarters in the rear
PS I offer no apologies for the state of the house.

GRAB THIS HOUSE AND HUG IT!
Quiet New Age fellow who gets in all manner of strife offers room for accommodation and uncoordinated dancing. Generally reclusive, wears no underwear, but leads a very exciting life. *Otherwise a normal, fun-loving bear.*
email address: H.B.Bear@paddedpaw.com

Adjectives for marketing your share-house

A airy, artistic, anarchist, agnostic, abundant, art deco, aged 20+, act now, activist, acid house

B beautiful, bushy, big, bright, bohemian, busy, bargain, B&D (bondage & discipline), broadminded (i.e. into sexual fetishes, serious drugs or queer)

C comfy, close to ..., communal, clean, cool, crusty, cosmopolitan, control freak, considerate, cosy, cheap, convenient, cyber-punk, calm, creative, crap

D desirable, dishwasher, dodgy, delightful, dog-lover, deviant, drug-free, drug-fucked, DTE (down to earth)

E eclectic, easy-going, environmentally aware, exotic, egotistical

F fun, friendly, funky, functional, feral, fantastic, fully furnished, freakish, filthy, free-range, financially stable, feng shui

G great, gorgeous, groovy, ga-roovy, gay-friendly, grrls, goth, GSOH (good sense of humour)

H happy, homey, hedonistic, house-trained, hippy, house-proud, honest, hygienic, a home not just a house, herbal

I independent, intelligent, intuitive, inspired, industrial, immaculate, into heavy metal, into recycling (etc.)

J joyous, jazzy, jewel-in-the-crown

K kindred spirits, kooky, krazy

L light, literary lovers, lefty, leafy, love-shack

M mature, minimal dogma, musical, meat eaters, modern, motivated, marble fireplace

N newly established, New York–style warehouse, nerd, New Age, non-smoker, non-racist, non-homophobic, no drama queens, no yuppies (etc.), normal, nudist

O organised, OFP (open fire places), OSP (off-street parking), organic, open-minded, out-going, occupied person

P post-modern, Paris end, polished floorboards, professionals, philosophical, peaceful, party-animals, pets okay, pretentious, psychic

Q quiet, queer, quaint

R relaxed, responsible, ravers, radical, recycled, reliable, retro

S single white female, spacious, skeptical, sporty, sunny, serial-sharer, smokers okay, sociable, sexy, sensitive, spiritual

T together, tidy, talkative, technophile, trippy, TV-addict, TS (transsexual), tragic

U unique, upmarket, unremarkable

V vegetarian, vegan, vegie garden

W warm, wonderful, witty, well-maintained, warehouse, wacky, warrior princess wanted

STEP 2 – THE PHONE CALL

The phone call should be used as a screening process so you don't have to waste your time meeting people who don't match your requirements. Some houses skip this step and just ask people to drop by for an interview. They are either brave or stupid. If you don't like the sound of someone, have an excuse prepared so you don't have to meet them. For example, ask them if they have much house furniture. If they say no, tell them that you are looking for someone with lots of furniture; if they say yes, tell them there's no more room.

STEP 3 – THE INTERVIEW

House interviews vary in length and formality. Usually they start with a guided tour and a viewing of the room. Sometimes the interview might take place standing around in the backyard and other times it might be like an interrogation panel with people taking notes and asking you to repeat that for the benefit of the tape. Some households will require a second or even a third interview. The style of the interview gives you an idea of what the people are like. If they are intimidating and nasty at the interview, they'll probably be nasty to live with and will chop you up if you die, like in the film *Shallow Grave*.

Being an interviewee can be a bit scary, especially if you find yourself surrounded by a whole household firing questions at you. It is especially hard at times when demand for households outstrips supply, as often happens in February at the start of the uni year. Try not to get so nervous that you lose your capacity for critical assessment.

SAFETY AT SHARE-HOUSE INTERVIEWS

Interviews can be risky when you are interviewing or being interviewed alone. For interview safety:

➪ arrange to meet your prospective housemate at a cafe rather than at the house

➪ take a friend or have a friend there

➪ ask for a reference, and ring the reference too – make sure they are who they say they are.

Interview questions

For many people, the key question that reveals someone's true personality is this: 'What kind of music do you like?' If the household is all into Metallica but the interviewee says *The Sounds of the Scottish Highlands*, the interview will be abruptly terminated.

The best way to find out what someone is like is to ask lots of detailed questions. Get them to be specific. You might seem a bit picky, but it's better to seem daggy at interview than risk moving in with someone who is a duck-shooting, sword-dancing, National Party voter if you're not. Here are some ideas:

⇨ Why are you moving out of your current house?/Why is the previous housemate moving out?

⇨ How would you describe your standard of cleanliness? How often do you like to do the dishes/vacuuming/cleaning the bathroom, etc.?

⇨ What do you do? (Work, study, etc.)

⇨ When you are at home, how do you usually spend your time?

⇨ Do you have a partner? How often would they be staying over?

⇨ How often would you have friends over?

⇨ How would you describe your personality?

⇨ How would you describe your politics and/or religious beliefs?

⇨ What drugs do you use and how often?

⇨ What are your TV watching habits?

⇨ What things do you really hate in a share-house?

⇨ Do you have any unusual habits around the house?

⇨ Are you a lazy slob / serial killer / pretentious prat?

For interviewees

⇨ How do you organise shopping and cooking?

⇨ Do you have a kitty – how much is it?

⇨ Do you sit down for meals together or not?

⇨ Do you have any rules or house agreements?

⇨ Would you expect the person who moves in to be on the tenancy agreement or not?

⇨ Who is on the tenancy agreement and who will I be paying rent or bond to?

(See chapter 3 for information on your legal status as a co-tenant, sub-tenant or lodger.)

Interview tales

I went for this house interview and they never bothered to show me around the house. There were three of them and they had three of their friends over. They were these glamorous women, they treated me like the little fool. I felt really uncomfortable. One of the housemates said, 'This is a typical example of our house. You can observe us and if you like what you see, then maybe you can move in.' So they just left me to sit there and watch them crap on to their friends. It was so rude, I just left.

— Lisa

One time we advertised in the paper and interviewed twenty-five people in one day. We had a bottle of vodka. It was very efficient, I'd show them the room, then ask if they liked it — if not, there's no point keeping them in the house. Some people want to sit and chat even though they don't want the room. It's a sliding scale — after you've had a bad one, the others don't seem as bad. People always say they can cook but it ends up being pasta with Dolmio sauce. We had one guy who played four horn instruments. Another guy came to the interview with his c.v. and his photo album, and he showed us photos of him and his mates playing cricket and going to the Big Day Out. One woman who came took one look at our house and said, 'It makes me appreciate the house I'm in now.'

— Mia

⇨ My last housemate was a real whinger, but he's really sorry now.

⇨ Can you lend me forty dollars?

⇨ I was boiling my underwear long before it became trendy.

⇨ I think Jesus would have lived here.

⇨ I'm very relaxed and I like to be free with my body.

⇨ I can't wait to introduce you to my rabbits – Fluffy, Daisy, Jenny, Muffy, Toodles, Blacky, Socks and Satan.

Interview detective work

Just about everyone (even the most revolting and bad-tempered person) will say at the interview: 'I'm into being clean and organised and I like to have open communication in the house.' Don't believe a word of it. Most people lie at interviews. When Fox Mulder and Dana Scully first met at a house interview, Mulder intuitively detected Scully's workaholism, obsessive note-taking and the underlying sexual tension between them. Meanwhile, Scully scientifically detected Mulder's paranoia, his weird web-fingered friends and his belief in the cleaning fairy. It was a case of 'forewarned is forearmed'.

⇨ Visualise: Remind yourself that you could be negotiating bills with this person, sharing meals, watching TV shows together, and seeing them in pyjamas (or naked) and hungover in the morning. Visualise spending the whole day at home with them. Does the thought of it make you feel happy, nervous or depressed?

➪ **Take a friend**: A friend can help with the assessment. Interviewers should keep them in the next room, in hearing range. If you are the interviewee, some households will see it as a bit strange if you arrive with a friend. You can simply lie and say they are dropping you off somewhere after the interview.

➪ **Pick up on the signs**: Did their questions focus on your personal interests or on cleanliness? Or did they just ask about your appliances? Beware of TV junkies who blew up their last set with overuse – all they care about is getting a TV owner to move in ASAP.

➪ **If you are the interviewer, don't give too much away**: Some interviewers start the house interview by telling the potential housemate exactly what they are looking for in a housemate. Instead ask the potential housemate what *they* want in a house. This way, they can't just parrot what you've already told them.

➪ **If you are the interviewee, check out the state of the house**: Does the level of cleanliness match your own? Don't be fooled if they say the house is usually much cleaner. If they offer you a cup of coffee, try and have a perv into their fridge when they're getting out the milk. The state of the fridge is symbolic of the state of the household generally.

➪ **Ask for another meeting**: If you are unsure, see if you can go back before you make your decision. This is not an unusual practice. Any doubts at the first interview are usually confirmed or dispelled at a second meeting. If you are the interviewee who is offered the room, say you'd like to come back first and have another look at the room. At the second meeting, think of some more specific questions that will address any doubts you may have had.

➪ If you can afford to, keep looking. Don't move in somewhere you don't feel positive about – it's not worth it.

Excuses if you want to leave

Sometimes as soon as the potential housemate opens the door and you see his socks pulled up under his roman sandals, you instantly know you don't want to live there. But how can you get out without having to go through the whole rigmarole? Well, honesty is one way. Or you could try:

➪ 'My friend's waiting for me in the car – I'll have to get going.'

➪ 'I don't think I'll fit my Yamaha organ in that bedroom.'

➪ Or the old standard: 'I'm the Australian BMX cross-country champion and I need a bigger backyard to practise in.'

STEP 4 – THE OFFER TO MOVE IN

Sometimes the housemates offer the room to you at the interview, but the most common practice is the 'don't call us, we'll call you' method. The interviewers get your phone number and let you know how long it will take to make a decision. When you don't hear within that time, you can assume you weren't successful. If you are offered a house that you don't like, the usual practice is to lie and say, 'Sorry, I've already found a place.'

Moving-in day

The exciting day has arrived. You are moving into this great new house with these fantastically exciting housemates. Now your life is going to be one big party ...

Pagan witch

She would sleep in the hallway, she was bit peculiar. She said she was a witch and a pagan and all that stuff. One night there was a full moon and she painted some eggs with her menstrual blood to worship the moon goddess, which is perfectly okay with me, but she put them in the bathroom cupboard. I had gone looking for some soap or something and there's these eggs in her menstrual blood and I've gone, 'No, it's really time to move out.' I stepped up my efforts to find a place. Just before I moved out she took up oil painting. Within about two days she did these six huge canvases of vaginas and stuck them up all over the lounge room. They were massive — a metre and a half square. Six vaginas around the lounge room. I moved out a couple of days later.

— Liana

Spider couple

This couple I was living with decided to go up north for a month. About a week before they were due to leave, I said I was going to do a really big clean-up around the house. They didn't seem to like what I was saying. There were all these massive spider webs in the kitchen. I knew they had a really strong connection to them, but they were really grating at me. I said, 'Right, okay, I'm going to get rid of these spider webs.' They started shouting at me: 'You can't get rid of them, they are part of the house.' I'm not saying that I am a spider hater, but I just got a horrible feeling when I went into the kitchen and saw about ten spiders in their webs. They decided not to go away after that — I think they were too worried about the spiders.

— Kevin

HOW TO BE POPULAR IN A SHARE-HOUSE

▷ **Appear to have an active sex life**: You will seem more attractive. Arrive home after your housemates are in bed. Make loud giggling noises and thump the bedroom wall. At 5 a.m., open and shut the front door. The next day, act smug but tired, say: 'God, I'm so shagged.' Do this at least six times per week.

▷ **Say you are in therapy (even if you aren't)**: But don't tell your housemates why you are going. Everyone will think of you as a complex individual with mysterious deep psychological issues to think about. You can also use this to get out of things you don't want to do: 'Sorry, I can't change the toilet roll. I really can't talk about it.'

▷ Better still, **become a counsellor**: Make reference to psychological theories. If anyone implies you are not doing enough cleaning, say 'I think you'll find you have an undiagnosed obsessive compulsive disorder. You should see a counsellor.' Other housemates will come to you with their problems, which gives you the opportunity to reinforce their inadequacies in a kind and helpful way. It also provides you with vital information — if one housemate has fallen in love with another, you will be the first to know.

⇨ **Act busy**: Never lounge around reading or watching TV. Make phone calls, whip up a chocolate mud cake, iron your party clothes. People will be impressed if your life seems an incredible whirl of activity. And any problems housemates have with you will never be raised – you will always be rushing out the door.

⇨ **Create a winning team**: Make veiled comments to other housemates, about one housemate in particular. Never directly backstab (this would not be nice), be patronising instead. Say: 'She sure does love cleaning. I guess she doesn't have much else to do in her life.'

⇨ **Make out you are wildly popular**: Leave messages on the answer machine from 'friends' saying there's a party Saturday night, everyone says it will be boring if you're not there. Have flowers arrive for yourself that say, 'Thank you so much. Even the doctors say that if it wasn't for you the cancer wouldn't have gone into remission.'

⇨ **Act important**: Change the conversation to focus on you. If everyone is sitting around watching the news, make an announcement about yourself. For example, 'I might have to have my left arm removed' or 'I had lunch with Olivia Newton-John.'

Chapter 9

Did someone say roster?

You've just moved into your new house and you're all still in the honeymoon phase, doing the dishes, talking to each other and watching TV together. So how do you share fairly and prevent a descent into chaos?

HOUSE AGREEMENTS

Agreements are the way forward. No more mucking about wondering if you're the only one who's ever scrubbed the toilet. When you've made an agreement about who will do what, you have a clearer idea of what to expect of each other. Agreements are best made when the house is established or when someone new moves in.

Some people don't believe in house agreements or rosters. At the very mention of a roster or a household rule these free-thinkers will make you feel like you're some kind of rigid Brownie-pack leader. But agreements reduce conflict. For example, if you all agree never to wash dishes and simply live off paper plates, then no one has to worry about being told off by a clean freak.

The idea of making agreements in a share-house has been supported by a recent New South Wales report that looked at tenancy legislation (*The Fair Share*, 1998). The report recommended that share-houses should be encouraged to develop agreements covering matters such as payments of bills, rent and ways of resolving disputes. While these would not be binding, it was suggested that they could be used to assist a tenancy tribunal to resolve disputes between tenants.

The following are some common agreements that can help to ensure smooth household interactions. Use the agreement form at the end of this chapter to write down what you decide on. To keep your agreements relevant and useful they should be reviewed every three to six months.

COMMON AGREEMENTS

1. Notice to vacate

It may seem strange to discuss leaving when you've just moved in, but this is an important issue. If one tenant wants to leave, how much notice should they give the others? In most states and territories, tenancy legislation does not cover how much notice co-tenants should give if one decides to leave, so it's particularly important to discuss this early. (However, in a sub-letting situation, head tenants and sub-tenants do have legal obligations regarding the amount of notice on leaving – see chapter 12.)

One month's notice is a common standard for co-tenants, as it gives the remaining people a reasonable amount of time to find someone new. Agree on the vacating person's responsibilities. This could include cleaning their bedroom, making sure anything they've damaged in the house is fixed, and allowing prospective new tenants to view their room, as well as informing the landlord or agent.

2. Kicking someone out

It is worth establishing house rules about under what conditions someone would be asked to leave. These might include:

⇨ failure to pay for rent or bills

⇨ deliberate damage to the house or the property of the housemates

⇨ violence, intimidation or harassment

⇨ repeatedly not sticking to household agreements.

3. Boudoir bargaining

In general, rent is divided by the number of occupied bedrooms in the house (i.e. if there are four people sharing a four-bedroom house, then the rent is divided equally by four). However, when the bedrooms in a share-house are considerably different in size and amenities (ensuites, balconies, walls, views) it is fair practice for those with the crappy bedrooms to pay less and those with luxuries like windows to pay more. The amount is usually a nominal $5 to $10 a week. There are always those who will make it their mission to get the best room in the house while insisting that everyone pay the same amount. They may argue that 'we all use the same lounge, bathroom, etc', but this is not a decent argument.

For couples who share just one bedroom, a common practice is that they pay slightly more than if only one person were living in that bedroom, in recognition that two people take up more room in the house.

4. Tips for dealing with the bills

⇨ Most bills (except STD and other phone calls) are equally divided between housemates. But if, for example, one housemate is growing dope plants under special lights in their wardrobe, or plays PlayStation for eighteen hours a day, it's only fair that they pay more for electricity.

⇨ Try to get every housemate's name put on each bill account, so that the responsibility is shared. If you can't do this, each person could put their name on at least one bill account. The person whose name is on the bill will be held liable if it is unpaid.

⇨ Sometimes phone, gas and electricity companies charge a connection fee. They may also request a bond, which is refunded when you move out (provided there is no money owing on the bill). Make an agreement on how to pay these bonds back if one tenant moves out. Often the new tenant who moves in pays the outgoing tenant their share of the bond. Keep records of any money paid between tenants, and make sure that receipts are given.

PHONE BILLS — THE WORST BILLS OF ALL

⇨ If everyone makes similar numbers of local calls, it is less stressful to just divide the local phone bill by the number of housemates. You could each keep a record of how many local calls you have made. This never works out exactly, but it can give you a general guide to the percentage of calls that people make, and you can divide the bill accordingly.

⇨ New technologically advanced ways of tracking calls might help. In their quest for any new marketing angle since privatisation, phone companies have caught on to the fact that people share-houses. Now you can request itemised bills for local calls. There is also a new system where housemates have a separate phone record each, and a separate phone number which produces a different ring. Contact your phone company to find out more – they'd love to hear from you.

> *We had a gold-star system for paying the bills. It started as a joke and then everyone became really competitive to get the gold star for paying their bills first.*
>
> *– Elise*

5. Communal or not

You don't have to live in a commune to be communal. In common share-house language, a communal household is one where everyone shares food costs and cooks for each other. Communal houses only work if everybody is committed to the sharing spirit. If you decide to have a communal household, agree on how often you will cook for each other (for example, you could share meals on weekdays, and cook for yourselves on weekends).

6. Hello kitty

A kitty is a common but strangely kindergartenish name for the money housemates contribute each week for communal household food costs. When the kitty includes food for meals, the amount is usually $20 to $50 each. An alternative is the mini-kitty, where you contribute $5 or $10 for the essentials like bread, milk and toilet paper, but you buy the rest of your food individually and each have your own shelf in the fridge.

7. Shop to the top

Often when houses are established, they'll develop a house shopping list of the agreed items that are to be bought out of the kitty money, and a system for sharing out who does the shopping each week. If you are the one who always mysteriously seems to get stuck with doing the shopping more than anyone else, reward yourself with a Bertie Beetle or similar delicacy.

8. Housework rosters

The great thing about housework rosters is that they provide a structure for accountability. You know who's meant to be doing what. Here are some common types.

HOME ZONES

This simple system is preferred by those who hate rosters. Divide the house cleaning into areas or zones such as floors (includes vacuuming and washing), cleaning the kitchen (includes fridge) and bathroom (includes toilet). Each person has an area that they are responsible for keeping clean.

CYCLICAL 'CONTROL FREAK' ROSTER

Suitable for larger households.

Housework type	Week 1	Week 2	Week 3	Week 4
Vacuuming the cat	Bert	Ernie	Felix	Oscar
Removing dead rats	Ernie	Felix	Oscar	Bert
Getting new beans for the bag	Felix	Oscar	Bert	Ernie
Drawing up the roster	Oscar	Bert	Ernie	Felix

LUCKY-DIP ROSTER

Found in wacky households that give names to their indoor plants. Write down household tasks. Place pieces of paper into a hat and each pick out a task. Have a new draw from the hat once a month.

SOMETHING-TO-DECLARE ROSTER

This is an excellent way to catch people who are not doing their share of the cleaning. Write down on a calendar whenever you complete a household chore. Once a month, hold an inquisition where you tally up who has done the most tasks. Those who have fallen behind are made to feel guilty and bad. Those who are ahead are lavishly praised.

A FEW WORDS ABOUT 'STANDARDS'

People do have different standards of messiness and hygiene. Some people don't rinse froth off dishes, while others fail to notice that the lounge-room rug is moving all by itself. However shocking and appalling these things may seem to you, you do have to find a compromise. Discuss and agree on general cleanliness standards. This is not being anal. It is simply establishing a basic sense of decency in the house.

THE DIRTY DISHES

The dishes can be the focal point for the share-house power struggle. One housemate may insist that dishes be done immediately after every meal, even breakfast, while another will let them collect for a month. You can often tell who has the power by whose dish-doing standards rule in the house.

The most basic guideline is that the housemate who bothers to make everyone a delicious 2-Minute noodle dinner does not have to do the dishes. Consider the following rules. *It's your turn to do the dishes when:*

➪ your housemate cooks for you

➪ you cook for yourself

➪ you invite friends over for dinner, even if your housemate eats dinner with you.

> I've got a guy friend who moved in with this girl, and he was trying to describe to me what an ultra-clean freak she was, and I went, 'Oh yeah, heard it all before.' And he said, 'No, when she cleans the tiles above the kitchen sink, she doesn't just clean them, she regrouts them.' He was totally serious — she would put new grout between the tiles all the time.
>
> — Nada

People don't share-houses in Japan. I find some things here very difficult. In Japan we rinse the dishes, but nobody here does. One time I argued with my housemate. He was a real healthy guy, into yoga. He didn't rinse. I told him it's not good for your body, all those soap suds.

— Tomo

9. Decision making

How you will decide things can become a big issue, especially for major decisions, like kicking someone out, moving someone in or getting a pet. Two possible ways to make group decisions are by consensus or by majority rule. With majority rule, most people get their way, but those that don't agree are forced to put up with others' decisions. With consensus, everyone has to agree before any action is taken. This ensures that everyone is happy with every decision, or is at least prepared to accept a decision despite their concerns.

10. House meetings

In share-houses where there are no regular house meetings, you know that something's up when someone decides to organise one. But house meetings don't have to be ominous. Agreeing to meet regularly (for example, once every two or three months) provides a set-aside time to raise problems and helps to prevent those awkward situations where you have to try to find the right moment to approach your housemates. If there are no problems, house meetings provide an opportunity to have a drink or a meal together as a household. It's a good idea meet at the pub or somewhere away from the house — being out of the home environment can give you a different

▷ Did someone say roster?

perspective. A useful house-meeting procedure is for everyone to take turns to say whether they are having any problems with anything. If there is conflict, try to stay focused on coming up with a solution rather than getting bogged down in blame. See chapter 10 for more on dealing with conflict.

We played Enya at the house meeting

For two years, I lived with three friends in what can only be described as a highly regimented, militaristic-style household, which was nevertheless based on a consensus decision-making model. Three of us were slobs and one of us, Penny, was borderline obsessive about cleaning (she Mr Sheen-ed her bedroom every Saturday). We knew we needed to communicate fairly regularly to ensure our friendship didn't suffer, so to do this we had regular house meetings which involved a rotating chairperson and secretary. A week before the meeting, the agenda would be stuck to the fridge and household members could add to it throughout the week. After the meeting, the draft minutes were posted for five days, during which time members could dispute the resolutions recorded. After this period, the final copy of the minutes was distributed and referred to at the next meeting. They were also referred to in daily life. I once incorrectly stacked the dishwasher. I put a large dish inside it which exceeded size specifications as set down in a previous meeting. I was shown the minutes outlining the relevant resolution and had to amend my dishwasher-stacking behaviour.

After a while, we found the meetings were getting a bit tense and negative. We addressed this by playing Enya during the course of the meeting, and by having a compulsory agenda item known as 'positive affirmations' where we each had to say something positive about the household.

I still can't believe I lived in this household and that I am still friends with all three housemates.

— Luce

House meetings from hell

We often had house meetings where this one guy who thought he controlled the house would tell us how much toilet paper we should be using, saying, 'You only need to use three squares.' There were three women living in the house. One of the women said, 'This just proves what a misogynist you are. You don't know anything about women.'

— Ana

The footballer used to spend a great deal of time on the toilet. The toilet was the only place we'd be able to pin him down while he was awake. If we ever had to discuss something, like who was going to get some toilet paper or whatever, we'd just go into the toilet and stand around and have this house meeting while he was doing his business. House meetings were just short discussions on which pub we were going to, or the fact that a wall had fallen down. If you came home and you were looking for people you'd find them in the toilet.

— Siobhan

11. House communication books

House communication books provide a place to record phone messages or the number of phone calls you each make, ask favours, note when bills are due, and inform each other of local phenomena (for example, 'I think the neighbour's house is on fire').

12. Partners and bathroom rights

When your new housemate moves in, you may discover that their partner has practically moved in too. Have an agreement about how often partners can be there (for example, a maximum of three days or nights per week). If they stay over often, discuss whether they should make some contribution to the house (this could range from buying some milk every once in a while to paying a regular portion of kitty or bills).

Bathroom rights are another consideration. Partners could be given lower bathroom rights than housemates (so that you're not late for work waiting for your housemate's boyfriend to finish his aromatherapy bath).

13. Guests, dossers and freeloaders

Nothing sours housemate harmony as fast as the festering guest. We all know the type. It's the friend or relative of your housemate who eats all the food, makes hundreds of phone calls and stays for months on end. The best thing to do is to agree to a time limit on how long visitors can stay and what is a fair contribution to the kitty and bills. Your agreement should also say that housemates are responsible for the actions of their guests and might also cover where in the house visitors can stay (is sleeping on the couch okay, or should guests stay in the bedroom of the housemate who invited them?).

14. No-sex rule

Some naïve households have a rule that there will be no sex between housemates. But anyone who thinks they can make a house law to stop sex is kidding themselves. Imagine: you're just about to kiss your housemate for the first time when he says, 'Oh no, we can't do this – what about The Rule.' It's unrealistic. Go for it, and worry about working out who will move out later.

15. No-smoking/no-drugs/ no-junkies rules

Have an agreement about where people can and can't smoke (for example, can you smoke in your own bedroom, in the lounge, or outside?). You could also consider agreements about other drug use in the house.

In share-houses, there's lots of talk about the need for no-junkie policies. But realistically, many heroin users don't fit the junkie stereotype and are not going to steal your CDs. And anyway, at a house interview you probably won't know if someone's a junkie because they won't tell you. It is true that any major addiction (drugs, gambling, stamp collecting) that's beyond a person's financial means could affect their ability to pay rent and bills. A less discriminating rule could be that anyone who can't pay rent or bills or who steals someone else's stuff will be asked to leave. Make this clear at the house interview. Another rule to consider might be whether people can use in the house or not.

⇨ Did someone say roster?

16. Other agreements to consider

⇨ **Pets**: All housemates to agree before a new pet is introduced to the house.

⇨ **Noise**: All housemates to agree about what hours noise is acceptable.

⇨ **Communication**: Decide whether housemates should let each other know if they are not coming home.

Rosters rule

The house was green all the way, you couldn't even buy Vita Brits because of the packaging. They'd have all these valerian teas, so it smelt like someone had vomited in the cupboard. One time this woman moved in who was really nervous about cooking. She picked a Saturday night to cook her first meal, which was the worst night to do it with so many people there. She was so stressed out. She was making pizzas all afternoon, had tins of food everywhere, tinned tomatoes, tinned artichoke hearts, kidney beans. This other housemate Ken kept walking in and telling her off for using tinned food. I got told off for having Pert 2-in–1 shampoo instead of the organic co-op shop shampoo that you have to pump out into a jar.

– Lisa

Some of our house rules included that all cleaning products must be lemon-scented (according to Marianne, they cleaned more effectively), the grill must cleaned by ten o'clock on a Friday night and the sponge that was to be used for the toilet was to be identified by cutting it into the shape of a 'T' (this was to prevent someone unwittingly using the toilet sponge for the bathroom basin). We also had rostered jobs including 'daily couch pillow fluffer', 'junk mail tidier' and 'CD straightener'.

— Georgie

Rosters are always canned — people say rosters never work, and everyone takes on the complete adult attitude, 'Well, if it needs to be done it will be done.' But that doesn't work in bloody share-houses. I found that being a woman, men don't notice a lot of stuff. That's a convenient cop-out 'cause they've never had to do a lot. You know, just like dusting, things that I would get freaked about because I'd think, oh my god, the time that it takes to do that. But then men wouldn't even think that it needs to be done. There is a sort of trivialising of a lot of stuff that does have to happen, and the bloody fairies don't do it.

— Rachael

SHARE-HOUSE AGREEMENT FORM

RENT

The date rent is to be paid on is ....

The rent for each bedroom is:

Bedroom 1 .... Bedroom 2 ....

Bedroom 3 .... Bedroom 4 ....

BOND

Total amount ....

1   Share $[amount] ....

    paid by [tenant's name] ....

    to .... on [date] ....

2   Share $[amount] ....

    paid by [tenant's name] ....

    to .... on [date] ....

3   Share $[amount] ....

    paid by [tenant's name] ....

    to .... on [date] ....

4   Share $[amount] ....

    paid by [tenant's name] ....

    to .... on [date] ....

BILLS

[Tenant's name] .... responsible for gas bill

[Tenant's name] .... responsible for electricity bill

[Tenant's name] .... responsible for water bill

[Tenant's name] .... responsible for phone bill

Cooking

Arranged by   ❑ roster   ❑ own arrangements   ❑ other

Details: . . . .

. . . .

Kitty

$[amount] . . . . each per week

due on [day due] . . . .

Shopping

Arranged by   ❑ roster   ❑ own arrangements   ❑ other

Details: . . . .

. . . .

Chores and cleaning

Arranged by   ❑ roster   ❑ area   ❑ other

Details: . . . .

. . . .

House meetings

Held on (e.g. the last Friday of every second month) . . . .

. . . .

. . . .

Moving out

The required amount of notice to vacate is: . . . .

. . . .

The conditions under which someone can be asked to leave

include: . . . .

. . . .

GUESTS AND PARTNERS POLICY

....

....

....

OTHER AGREEMENTS

....

....

....

AGREEMENT SIGNATORIES   DATE

....

....

....

....

MORE HOUSEMATES FROM HELL

He was from Canberra

I am from Malaysia, so when I moved to Australia, I thought I should get to know the culture. I decided to try sharing a house. I moved in with these two guys, one Australian and one Japanese guy. The Japanese guy he's a student, he's a bit dodgy, he is walking around in a mechanic's outfit. He's not a mechanic, he's a bloody student. He says he's vegetarian but last week I saw him cooking pork sausage at 3 a.m. He is a bit weird, he's got a big lock on his bedroom door. The other guy, Greg, he is a bit of a funny guy too. One night I walk into the lounge and he is watching TV wearing an Ethiopian costume with a headdress and everything. He is a white guy, from Canberra.

— Azahr

Loin

I lived in this house in Hobart. One of the guys I lived with had lank greasy hair, long at the front and long at the back, like a variation of the mullet, and carried these kali beads everywhere. He'd wear sheepskin boots, army pants and this flannel shirt with the Luke Skywalker tuck. He was into paganism. He walked around with a staff. He would come into the room and put his staff in the corner of the room. He had shrines in the garden, totems and sticks tied like the Blair Witch. One day we got locked out, so we got in through his bedroom window. We got blasted with this smell. Inside was this line strung across the room, with animal pelts strung up and dishes of salt on the ground and this smell of formaldehyde. There were animals like snakes in jars and bits of wood carvings and posters of men standing on the tops of mountains and stuff. We thought he was harmless, but one morning he got too friendly with Louise. She was sitting near the heater before work – winter in Hobart is freezing. Suddenly he comes into the room with nothing on but a loincloth. She was on the floor level, could see everything under the loincloth.

– Tom

One house I lived in was a nude house. I don't know why, we just sat around all day naked and watched TV. It wasn't sexual – it was like a nudist colony but no one spoke about it. When I moved in, no one had told me, I just took my clothes off and that was it, it was just what you had to do. We all sat around every day getting stoned, and watching Dogs in Space and Apocalypse Now on this video recorder we had flogged from a doctor's surgery. One girl who moved in was a psycho. She pulled a knife on one of my housemates. She did a runner when she left, she trashed the kitchen and wrote 'scum' on the walls. And she was a thief, she even stole the video recorder.

– Ed

Chapter 10

Share-house dilemmas

When French philosopher Jean-Paul Sartre said 'hell is other people' he must have been living in a share-house. The daily sharing of a living space and household tasks inevitably creates disagreements. Feelings of irritation and resentment are as common as milk crates in share-houses and yet resolving disputes in a share-house can be particularly difficult. Housemate relationships are different from those with workmates, families or partners in that it's harder to know what you should expect of each other, and you often have to agree about whether an issue is even negotiable before it can be discussed.

In some share-houses trying to discuss any problem is just not cool. If your housemate steals your TV, your only dilemma is whether to chop down their dope plants or blow up their bedroom. If you try to communicate your feelings, you may be treated like some kind of share-housewife. You may find yourself doubting your own perceptions and thinking that maybe you are just an anal social reject like your housemate reckons.

Most people hate confrontations and disagreements and avoid them like the pox. This can be particularly true for housemates who value the friendliness of share-houses. People tend either to learn to tolerate annoying habits and weird behaviour (which is not a bad thing) or stew for months before unexpectedly erupting in the kitchen one morning. Given the uncertainty, different expectations and personalities, it is not surprising that problems are not often talked about directly.

The actions that clearly cross the lines of acceptable housemate behaviour, such as stealing and rampant selfishness, are in some ways more straightforward to deal with. For everything else you have to find a way to be tolerant but also to get what you need from your share-house. While you may be able to get your housemate to modify their more objectionable habits, what you can't do is change their personality. Some share-houses will not suit you and some housemates are just a nightmare. There is nothing you can do.

When you feel yourself not coping, which happens more often than you might think in a share-house, don't be too proud to get some help. You could talk to a counsellor about it or go to a dispute resolution service.

The following approaches to common dilemmas have been tried and tested by many housemates in the past.

MULTIPURPOSE PROBLEM RESPONSES

The first question to ask yourself is how much the problem is really bothering you. You have to practise some tolerance and choose your battles, otherwise you won't last five minutes. There are some things that you will have to live with.

A direct and effective approach is to tell someone how you feel about their behaviour without attacking them personally. Being assertive is no guarantee for getting things your own way, but you do get to feel reasonable and fair. You also get your feelings out in the open rather than bottling them up. But being assertive is often not easy – it takes practice and confidence.

Level 1 – Occasional complaints

Maybe your housemate has not done his or her chores as agreed, or has woken you up at 4 a.m. crawling down the hallway. Probably your housemate doesn't realise that these things are bothering you. Simply let them know what you'd like them to do. For example: 'Do you think you could do the dishes?' or 'Can you be quieter at night?'

Level 2 – Feeling consistently irritated or upset

When there is a pattern of behaviour that you are feeling upset about or a conflict has developed between you and your housemate, you can get to the point where you always feel irritated in your own home.

1. You probably feel like shouting: 'You are a totally selfish bitch/bastard.' It is hard to avoid the temptation, but try to hold off. Maybe your housemate has different

expectations than you, or feels your standards are unreasonable. Even if you think they are lazy or thoughtless, blaming them will probably only get their back up and won't get the problem solved. Try to stay calm and focused on the problem.

2. Weigh up the situation. How and when will you approach them? How responsive have they been in the past? Are you in a good frame of mind to tackle the issue?

3. Approach them in a way that acknowledges their position. This can help to reduce defensiveness. For example: 'I know you've been stressed lately, but ...'

4. Tell them how their behaviour is affecting you. Try to focus on their behaviour rather than judging their entire personality.

5. Be persistent. Keep saying it until they listen.

6. Give them a chance to respond. Showing them that you are trying to understand their position can encourage them to listen to your own perspective. Be prepared to discover something that you didn't know before, like maybe they are pissed off with you about something too.

7. Focus on how you can both make things work better in future, rather than getting stuck on who did what. Let them know what you'd like them to do. If you can't come to an agreement, try to work out a compromise. You could arrange to discuss it again in a month's time, to see how things are going.

Level 3 – Ongoing conflict/major tension

Sometimes you may find yourself living with someone who doesn't care about resolving conflict, who believes they are never wrong, or who is uncompromising. You may have tried repeatedly to discuss things but they have not been resolved, and conflict and tension remain in the house. At this point your options are:

⇨ Stop trying to change your housemate's behaviour – change what *you* do. Change your house arrangements so that you do more things separately rather than jointly. For example, investigate getting separate phone numbers and billing systems.

⇨ Try to cope with the built-up frustration by whingeing to your friends, doing relaxation exercises, making your bedroom a place where you can spend your time or getting out of the house more.

⇨ Consider going to a dispute resolution service. Trained mediators can help you all sit down together, identify the issues and come up with possible solutions. Your housemates must be willing to participate in the mediation session with you. Often a dispute resolution service can give you advice over the phone before you move on to the next step of attending a mediation session. Advice from dispute resolution services is often free of charge.

⇨ Face up to the fact that it's not working, sooner rather than later. Weigh up the pros and cons of staying and leaving. Think about how living in the house is affecting you. Are you lying awake stressing out about the house? Are you avoiding going home? If you are feeling constantly stressed by living together it's time to move out or to kick someone out. You'll feel incredibly relieved and the world will be a brighter, happier place.

COMMON DILEMMAS

1. Dividing bills and levels of consumption

Next to dishes, money runs a close second to being at the root of share-house arguments. If you share-houses for long enough you will come across those who skip out without paying the bills, those for whom parting with money is like parting with their firstborn, and those who argue that they use less hot water than everyone else because they never shower.

In some situations it's fair to divide bills according to individual levels of consumption (power, food, etc.). The difficulty is that it's very hard to calculate who uses what or who eats what. Problems can also arise when there are differences in incomes. Someone on a low income might live by candle-light to reduce energy costs, while another housemate wants the place lit up like a 7–Eleven.

You'll need to sit down together and do some creative accounting. Start by discussing levels of consumption, taking into account in-kind contributions too – for example, if one person is eating a lot more of the shared food, perhaps that person could pay extra, or do more of the shopping as a contribution in kind.

2. My housemate is home all the time

You don't always want to have to deal with other people. Sometimes you want time alone or just time with your friends at home. If your housemate is always home, try approaching it as a common issue, for example, 'How about each of us having the house to ourselves one night a week?' But if your housemate doesn't have many friends or interests, there's not really much you can do. Perhaps you could take up a particularly irritating musical instrument like the violin and practise one night a week; suggest this could be their night out.

3. Feeling like the share-house slave

Probably the most common complaint in a share-house relates to disagreements about the division of labour. If you feel as though you are constantly putting in more effort than others, you'll quickly build up resentment.

You may be tempted to respond via non-verbal methods, such as leaving the vacuum cleaner in the lounge room for your housemate to trip over, putting their dirty dishes between their sheets or engaging in 'display cleaning', where you clean the kitchen in a loud and dramatic way for three days. But the trouble is, your housemates might not comprehend your non-verbal message, or may choose to ignore it.

Talking to your housemate directly about it is probably the most effective strategy. Tell them you feel like you are doing an unequal share and find out what their response is. Hopefully they will apologise, say they've just been busy lately and agree to put in more effort. But other likely responses are:

⇨ **THEY CLAIM THAT THEY ARE DOING MORE THAN YOU IN OTHER AREAS**

It is hard to know what contributions other people make, and maybe you are not noticing their efforts. Discuss and agree on what each person will do. You could consider a roster which you each tick off and date when a task is complete, so it's clear who is doing what.

➪ They don't see the effort you are putting in as necessary, because they have different standards

If this is the case, then it's a matter of compromising. You could consider a trade-off of tasks (for example, if you agree to do the vacuuming, they could be responsible for organising for the bills to be paid).

➪ They are a freeloading parasite

Naturally they won't admit to this, but you may suspect it anyway. But in the end, whether your housemate is being lazy or not is beside the point. If they don't see the situation as a problem but you do, all you can do is change your own actions. Make a list of all the chores you do and decide which ones are important to you (for example, cleaning the fridge) and which ones you will stop doing. You could do your own dishes and let theirs pile up or you could decide to cook only for yourself. Keep your bedroom clean so you feel you have somewhere to retreat to. The rest of the house might look like it's been ravaged by a cyclone, but at least you will save your energy for other things.

MEDITATION FOR HOUSEMATES WHO DO TOO MUCH

I am a beautiful person. I make an important contribution to our society.

My efforts must not be exploited.

4. My house has turned into a love shack

Public house-areas should not be used for sucky love talk or intimate moments. No one wants to witness someone else's love life in great detail or hear the pathetic names they have for each other. If they're hogging the couch and making you feel unwelcome in your own home, tell them how you feel. If a couple wants to call each other 'poochy-woo-woo', they'll have to live by themselves or go to their room.

A share-house named desire

When me and Kate got together, we didn't want the others to know because we thought it might wreck things. We'd sneak around the house after the others had gone to bed. It got pretty difficult – one morning one of our housemates got up early, and I had to get back to my room. I don't know what we were thinking but we had the brilliant idea that I would get dressed up in Kate's clothes. I put on her dressing gown and wrapped a towel around my head. I was just going to race past the other housemate's bedroom, so she'd only see a glimpse and think I was Kate. But I mistimed it and another housemate caught me charging down the hall in the pink dressing gown. She said, 'What are you doing in Kate's dressing gown?' I said, 'I'm just borrowing it' and ran off. Then this rumour got back to Kate that all the others thought I was a transvestite and was sneaking into the girls' bedrooms to dress up.

– Marcus

5. My housemate has a serious personal problem or illness

Living with someone who is depressed, unwell, has a serious addiction or has some other major emotional problem can be really stressful.

You don't have to become your housemate's friend or their counsellor. You can show concern, and ask them if there is anything you can do to help, but be clear about what you can and can't do.

If their problem is making you unhappy in the house, talk to them about it. Say that although you are concerned, you are finding it difficult to live with. Being direct about their problem can encourage them to realise they need help.

If you feel pressured to support them more than you can, suggest they talk to a counsellor or a friend. You could ring Lifeline, Suicide Help Line or a mental health service yourself for ideas and support.

6. I've fallen in love with my housemate

When living in close quarters with other people, there's always a risk of great love or great hatred. The way your housemate jumps on the overstuffed rubbish bin can be so alluring. If you are single, sharing can be an opportunity for finding love – if not your housemate then maybe one (or two) of their friends.

Desire is risky in a share-house. If by some bizarre chance your housemate love-object does not reciprocate, you'll have to live with the rejection every day. If you do get together, your other housemates might not appreciate the change in dynamics. And having your other housemates gossip about you can totally ruin your 'honeymoon phase'. So be prepared to move out if you do get together long-term, or if things don't work out.

When considering an in-house relationship, the first thing to do is suss out the other person's level of interest in you. Try this four-step test:

⇨ Raise the subject of their 'love life'. Are they interested in anyone else, or do they make allusions to an unmentioned person (who could be you)?

⇨ Stay up late watching home-shopping shows. Do they stay up late with you? This may be a good sign.

⇨ Are they averse to your germs? Offer them a taste of something off your spoon.

⇨ Watch for changes in appearance. Have they stopped hanging around the house in ugg boots? Are there new leopard-print G-strings on the line or is your love-object still hanging out ancient bog-catchers?

If the answer is yes to all of these questions, looks like you're on a winner. A common practice once you get together is to conceal the relationship in the early days. You'll have to get good at sneaking about. Don't risk telling one housemate – if you've told one, you'll have told them all. Keep the household interactions the same as usual. Don't start going bowling together and not inviting the other housemates or they'll start wondering why they're excluded (and probably why you've taken up bowling). And avoid excessive lying to your other housemates – they'll resent it when they finally find out.

7. Bad mood rising

Frequent moodiness is a form of selfishness. Not speaking for days, slamming doors, grumpiness, throwing tantrums – all these things suggest someone who is inconsiderate of the people around them. If you've had a bad day, keep your shittiness to yourself. If you're living with a grumpy bastard, you shouldn't be expected to tolerate it. Pick the time when they are in a good mood to talk to them about it. Tell them how their moods affect you, and ask them to stay in their bedroom or stay out of the house.

8. Living with a dictator

Some people believe that their way is right and seem to enjoy telling others what to do. What they ask you to do may not be unreasonable, but it's the *way* that they ask you. They expect obedience.

If a housemate starts giving orders, tell them you don't like the way they are speaking to you, and that you are going to ignore them if they speak to you like that again. They might stop this behaviour if they realise it isn't going to work or if they can see that they are being unreasonable.

I lived with this woman who acted as though she owned the house, like she was the parent and we were the lazy teenagers. She controlled everything — all the bill money had to be paid to her. She only had it like that so she could reprimand anyone who was a day late. She'd tell us off all the time in this shrill pompous voice: 'Who left that tap dripping?' or 'That's the second time I've had to tell you to turn the music down. I don't expect to have to tell you again.' You wanted to do the opposite, just to piss her off. We had a house meeting where we told her we didn't like being spoken to like children. She acted like we were being too sensitive. We couldn't ask her to leave because the owner was her friend, so we ended up moving ourselves.

– Tahnee

9. The socially challenged housemate

Socially challenged housemate behaviour can take all kinds of hideous forms. There's the common problem of the loud sex at 3 a.m. Some not only are suspected of failing basic toilet training 1.0, but appear unable to ever change the toilet roll. Then there are those who casually fart on the couch and leave their pubic hair in the soap.

Reclaim your right to live in a share-house where it is safe to sit on the toilet seat.

Fight back.

⇨ Refer to accepted national standards, e.g. 'Your behaviour is un-Australian.'

⇨ After a night of loud raucous shagging, let your housemate catch the end of your telephone call when you say '. . . last night they sounded like a herd of wild goats'.

⇨ Save up the empty toilet rolls. Make them into a sculpture, exhibit them and invite your housemate. Call it 'My Amazement At My Housemate's Total Selfishness'.

⇨ Spray them with air freshener.

⇨ Substitute the word 'people' for your housemate's name, e.g. 'Can people keep the noise down.' N.B. Don't try this if you live with just one other person.

⇨ Cry. Say: 'I just can't cope with the hairy plughole, I can't go on living any more.'

10. House rage

House rage is often the result of a major personality clash — you're nice and they're nasty. You know you've got the rage when your friends begin to get that 'not again' look on their face when you mention his or her name for the twentieth time that hour. It can wake you in the morning and stop you sleeping at night. With each passing day you add another 'crime' to your burning cauldron of hatred. Everything becomes their fault – the hassles from your case manager, the state of your bedroom, the fleas on your dog. Recognise the early warning signs – are you sticking pins in dolls or messing with their car brake cables? Channel the hatred creatively. Sing a song about your housemate or paint a picture of them (on their wall). The problem with house rage is that it can become a health hazard. There is only one guaranteed cure for house rage – stop living together.

MEDITATION FOR HOUSE RAGE

You and I are different. You are a hideous creature and I am not.

Share-house support group

MEETS EVERY TUESDAY NIGHT IN THE LOUNGE
(BYO cushion)

Are you struggling with ugly feelings of
bitterness and resentment towards your
housemates?
Do you feel like no one listens to you?
Come along to our support group for
housemates. We listen. We care.

THIS MONTH'S DISCUSSION TOPICS INCLUDE:

- CDs found in the wrong cover
- Crumbs left on the kitchen bench
- When a housemate has a contract out
  on you
- Effective bedroom barricades
- Living with country music fans
- When silence is a weapon
- Vinyl bean bags and other décor problems
- Housemates who chew too loudly
- Non-attendance at house meetings
- Wet bath mats

Refreshments and tranquil music provided.

Resentful moments . . .

If you ever did any cleaning in the house, José would basically just leave. I did a lot of bitching and didn't say a lot — you just think that they should know what to do. I'd bring the vacuum cleaner out and leave it in the middle of the lounge room. It makes you feel really shitty about yourself when you are putting up with something that you should say something about. He'd vacuum his own room and then put it away and not bother to do any of the rest of the place. Oh god, that really really shitted me to tears.

— Drea

They didn't like anything formalised, so you couldn't raise an issue. The house focus was group therapy, a refuge from the horrible outside world, and it does suck you in. They had expectations that were unrealistic of a housemate. Natasha would do the gardening and get resentful like we weren't doing enough, even though I regularly would be doing dishes and she never did them.

— Leigh

A few times I got myself worked up about things, but I would always try and soften the blow. I think in the end you sort of end up questioning yourself, thinking maybe it's something about me, maybe I'm just an unreasonable person, but we both had our moments bitching and door slamming and writing terse notes to each other.

— Annie

Chapter 11

Harmonise your household

Share-house dynamics tend to deteriorate over time. Even in the most caring and sharing household, the regular tolerating and negotiating thing can wear a bit thin. So how do you revitalise and harmonise your home?

A wise housemate once said: 'The house that plays together stays together.' While they were probably cheating at Monopoly at the time, there is some truth in this cliché. If the only time you talk to your housemates is to argue about who made the calls to dodgy 0055 numbers, then maybe you need to try some strategies to put the *fun* back into your *fun*ctional household.

SHARE-HOUSE VIDEO AND TV REVIEW

The household video night is a great way to create a little togetherness without actually having to talk to each other. Why not hire a video about share-houses? After all, you can all relate to this subject. Here is a review of share-house film and TV through the decades.

The straight sixties

In the 1960s, when there were few mixed-gender households, there was *The Odd Couple* (1967). This highly accurate analysis of the flatmate personality clash depicts two divorcee friends Oscar (Walter Matthau) and Felix (Jack Lemmon) who call each other by their ex-wives' names. Together they represent the yin (slob) and the yang (clean freak) of housemates, except that they don't complement each other. Highly recommended viewing for two-person households.

The sideburning seventies

In the 1970s, as mixed-gender sharing gained acceptance, there was *Man About the House*, which was still a bit risqué for its time. It involved a cranky landlord downstairs and two dippy birds sharing with a sleaze with the biggest sideburns you've ever seen. All very naughty.

The alternative eighties

The Young Ones was about a student house with bottom-burping boys Mike, Vivien, Ric and the house scapegoat, Neil the hippy. Their cruelty, pretentiousness, filfthy habits and extreme violence made it well worth watching. Anarchy meant staying up all night long. There are talking carrots, lots of snot and arguments over who has to sit on the rickety chair.

Then there was *Dogs In Space* set in Richmond (Melbourne) in pre-AIDS-awareness 1978 (but made in 1986), and seen by many Melbournians as the quintessential share-house film. Sammy (played by Michael Hutchence) and Anna (Saskia Post) live in a kind of share-house Noah's Ark – there's two of every species of punk, anarchist, engineering student, junky and brat. Michael Hutchence has a floppy hair problem and the props include a ridiculous number of VWs and bodies posed in crash position on the brown shag carpet.

The nasty nineties

Just when you thought share-houses couldn't get any more deviant, the 1990s revealed the more sinister aspects lurking under the thin veil of housemate civilisation.

In *Single White Female* (1992), Hedy (Jennifer Jason Leigh) appears to be the ideal roommate. She's not perfect, but then what housemate is? She kills her roommate's boyfriend and pushes her puppy out the window. But anyone who has ever shared a house can appreciate the effort she goes to in cleaning the flat before she moves out (she even goes as far as wiping off her fingerprints ...). The share-house meltdown takes the form of a rather intense confrontation in the basement. Inappropriate housemate behaviour ensues when Hedy strangles Ally (Bridget Fonda) in the elevator, and Ally knifes Hedy in the back a couple of times. It must have been the way that Hedy kept leaving the milk out of the fridge.

In *Reality Bites* (1993) the share-house is a backdrop for the signposts of a generation. There are crises about AIDS, unemployment, bills, careers, parental expectations and coming out. They dance in the 7–Eleven to 'My Sharona', film each other on hand-held video and sing in grungy bands. There's the obligatory Gen-X slacker who makes cleverly alienated remarks from the couch (Ethan Hawke), but it's not nearly demented enough for a share-house film. There's not enough drugs, there's no deaths and no murders, and the Winona Ryder character can ease her twenty-something angst with her high disposable income – who the hell can relate to this? And there's only one sex scene.

Shallow Grave (1994), set in Scotland, provides helpful ideas on how to conduct house interviews (interviewees are subjected to brutal assessments, Polaroids and a singing competition) and a rather gruesome share-house confrontation. The meltdown consists of Dave (Christopher Eccleston) trying to get out the door with all the loot from the dead housemate (isn't there always one). Dave and Alex (Ewan McGregor) wrestle on the kitchen table, which by the way is remarkably tidy for a house in conflict. Alex slams David's head in the refrigerator, and on and on it goes. Apparently this film is used as an instructional video for mediators at Edinburgh's share-house dispute resolution service.

In *The House from Hell* (an Australian TV and radio series) Andrew Denton tortures six mismatched people by putting them together in a Sydney house ... which begs the question, if they wanted to see odd people acting all crazed and demented, why didn't they just go round to any old share-house?

Queen Cat, Carmel and St Jude (ABC series) has three innocent country girls sharing in the big city. This *Anne of Green Gables* version of the share-house is about finding kindred spirits and discovering your true talents.

John Birmingham's popular book (and stage play and film) *He died with a felafel in his hand* chronicles the worst of share-house crimes and misdemeanours. If there was a database for dud housemates *Felafel* has all the raw material. And yet it gives hope to housemates right across the land – you too could become a legend in your own lounge room.

Just like an episode of *Friends* with a few more bucket bongs, drug busts and decomposing rats. *Felafel* was followed by Birmingham's book *The Tasmanian Babes Fiasco*.

This Life (1997 BBC series screened here on the ABC) is about yuppy lawyers sharing in London. *This Life* managed to make interesting viewing of common share-house arguments (dishes, hogging the bathroom, stuff being stolen), though we guess that not quite as much nakedness, shagging, jealousy, betrayal, psychoanalysis and ambition go on at your place. If it did, maybe you'd stay in more often.

The title of the US comedy *Friends* gives it away. They are all just so perky, quirky, friendly and well dressed. There's no lasting bitterness or big red pimples here. The cast is a tad skinnier than your average housemate and the apartment a bit more tidy. You may find yourself wondering whether if you moved the couch closer to the window and hung your bedspread on your wall, your place could sort of look like that.

Honourable mentions

Other series that include a sharing or boarding situation include *House Gang* (SBS series about people with disabilities sharing) and *Men Behaving Badly* (British series shown on the ABC) and on film, *Bedrooms and Hallways*, *Fight Club*, *Occasional coarse language*, *Notting Hill*, *Trainspotting*, *Career Girls*, *Love and Human Remains*, *Love and other Catastrophes*, *Pacific Heights*, *Monkey Grip*, *Withnail and I*, and *GoFish*.

And who can forget *Gone Like The Wind (With My CDs)*, *The Odd Angry Housemate*, *Guess Who's Coming To Dinner (Again)*, *10 Things I Hate About You*, *You've Probably Got Mail (But Your Housemate Has Hidden It)*, *The Share Witch Project*, *The DSS Always Ring Twice* and *The Sound Of Music (At 3 a.m. – Again)*.

FUN AND GAMES

If the telly's on the blink you may be forced to look at your housemates. Possibly you may even have to talk to them. To make it easier, why not join in some share-house entertainment? These suggestions can help to put the spark back into sharing and might even enable you to convey your secret desires or irritations in a subtle but effective way.

Dig out the crumpled *pack of 49 cards* with pictures of naked milkmen, make a few cheese sandwiches, pour some glasses of Jim Beam and blow a bit of smoke around for that authentic cards-night feel. Play *card kitty*, in which you bet with the kitty money. The person who loses goes without food for the week.

Have a *jam*. Grab your fun-loving housemates, a spoon and saucepan, the jar of lentils and somebody's school recorder and get down and make some noise. Or turn it into a *performance evening*. Housemates and their friends can develop little skits and present their Oscar-winning performances. Offer a lovely prize and your housemates will by dying to join in. And remember, any stupid activity will seem much more fun when combined with a *drinking game*.

For romance potential, why not try *Twister*, which has an inherent physical intimacy (i.e. your head nearly up their bum) that is especially good for seduction plans.

Not yet immortalised as a board game is the popular share-house activity *street sign scrummaging*. For detour signs and other portable road signs, score 5 points; street signs that were attached to poles (including no standing, give-way signs, etc.) score 7 points; stop signs score 8 points; unusual signs or signs from corporations or public services like K-Mart or library score 10 points; blue police signs score 50 points and an automatic teller machine scores the maximum 100 points.

Shopping trolley race is a great game for sporty housemates. This requires two or more stolen supermarket shopping trolleys and one sloping road. Highways are dangerous but more exciting. For *corridor cricket* you'll need a bat (rip up a floor board if you don't have one), a ball, two milk crates as wickets, a corridor and a few cherished items of your housemates to break when you hit a six.

Celebrate and join in the annual all-day *share-house festival*, in which stained and smelly couches are collected from nature strips. Also known as *hard rubbish day*.

Murder in the dark is also fun for housemates with repressed hatreds. Turn all the lights off and begin counting loudly backwards from 50; all your housemates must find a place to hide in the house or garden. Then you must go and 'murder' one of them, i.e. once you find one, you tap them on the shoulder and they are 'dead', then they become the murderer. The new murderer must then begin counting backwards from 50 and so on until you are completely bored out of your brain and call out, 'Can someone bloody come and murder me, *please*.'

Celebrity head (also known as *tally ho*) is an ideal game for getting a message to your housemate. You each write a famous person's name on the back of a cigarette paper, then lick and stick to your housemate's forehead. You take turns in asking questions to try to guess whose name you have on your head. The questions can only be answered yes or no, and any 'no' answer that you get means it is the next person's turn. Pick names with a theme such as Hitler, Gengis Khan, Margaret Thatcher and Jeff Kennett and your housemates will soon begin to receive your subliminal message.

Finally, the great *share-house Scrabble-off* is ideal for settling such moving-out disputes as who gets to take the telephone table that you all bought last year. Or use a

Scrabble-off to decide who must do the dishes that no one will own up to. It will improve your word skills while simultaneously resolving share-house disputes.

SPICE UP YOUR LIFE

Housemates invariably have different cooking standards. Sometimes all you want is 2-minute noodles but you feel compelled to whip up a great dish because your housemate has been cooking Royal Thai cuisine for the whole of the last century. When it comes to your turn, the crucial ingredients will have been eaten by some unknown person for breakfast. Not to worry. Here are some sure-fire share-house meals to cook when the kitty is bare. These recipes have lovingly been handed down from housemate to housemate.

The classic munchies

French onion dip: Your basic house-warming dish. Mix a packet of French onion soup with cream cheese, add a packet of biscuits and a party. N.B. Doubles as an ashtray and will still look fresh the next day with cigarette butts stuck in it.

Cheese à la toaste: Add sliced tomatoes and devilled eggs, whatever – the only limitation is your imagination. Tastes better in the wee small hours after a night of destroying your liver and your taste buds.

Kellogg's Variety packs: One nutritious meal for each night of the week – from Sultana Bran to Coco Pops.

Lentils: Every share-house has a jar of lentils that's been in the cupboard since 1975. Transport them through time to create a rather delicious lentil curry, soup, patties, casserole or dahl. Add onions, garlic, curry powder and any bit of leftover vegetable.

Pasta and tomato sauce: This one's for the connoisseurs. Cook up some pasta and add tomato sauce straight from the bottle. Don't add anything else – it ruins easily.

Green potato and pea curry: Dig out the frozen peas from the last millennium, add green potatoes, tinned tomatoes (or tomato paste), curry powder, onions and garlic. Cook it up and serve with rice.

Savoury popcorn: Add melted butter, grated parmesan cheese, a splash of soy sauce and half a clove of crushed garlic – you'll have it all to yourself.

Meals that require six ingredients or less
(not counting oil, water and onions – all vegetarian)

PASTA

1. Pasta (spaghetti, fettuccini, penne, bow ties – whatever is in the cupboard)
2. Sauce options

Red: Fry onion, crushed garlic and sliced red peppers. Add a can of tinned tomatos and a handful of chopped olives. Boil up some penne pasta and combine with the tomato mixture. To make it more exciting, put it all in a baking tray, put parmesan cheese and breadcrumbs on top and bake it in the oven.

Green: Fry onion, garlic, spinach (frozen is okay), basil pesto and some cheese. Add sour cream or yogurt to serve.

Brown: Fry onion, sliced mushrooms and garlic. Combine with sour cream, cream cheese, cream or chopped fetta. Serve with parmesan on top.

ROASTED VEGIES

1. Choose a range of vegetables. These could include potatoes, carrots, parsnips, pumpkin, corn on the cob (in quarters), red pepper, mushrooms, zucchini, eggplant (sliced lengthways and brushed with oil on both sides), onions (in quarters), garlic cloves (leave them whole in the skin for baking).

2. Place 1–2 tablespoons of oil in a baking tray and add the hardest vegies like potatoes, pumpkin, carrot, etc. Bake for ten to twenty minutes, then add other vegies and bake for about another half an hour. Baking temperature should be about 200–220ºC or 400–450ºF.

3. To roast the harder vegetables quicker, boil them first, dry them and then add with the other vegies in baking tray.

4. Sauce options: sprinkle with balsamic vinegar and oil or rosemary and salt about 5–10 minutes before vegetables are finished baking. Alternatively, serve with sour cream, mayonnaise, cheese, tomato sauce or sweet chilli sauce.

FORKS-HIGH STIRFRY

Fry some nuts (peanuts, almonds, cashews) in oil in a wok until browned. Remove the nuts from the wok and then heat up a bit more oil and add crushed garlic and 1 tablespoon of chopped ginger (optional). Fry up any mixture of vegetables (carrots, zucchini, green beans, mushrooms, bok choy, eggplant). When nearly cooked, add 1–2 tablespoons soy sauce, 1–2 tablespoons sherry and 1 teaspoon honey. Fry for two minutes. Sprinkle with nuts and serve on rice.

LAZY PERSON'S SOUP

You will need water, onion, a tin of tomatoes, garlic, any orange or green vegies, 1 teaspoon of basil and a dash of cinnamon and paprika. Feeling more energetic? Add a tin of chickpeas! Serve with bread and cheese.

Dessert: Self-saucing chocolate pudding

A favourite with housemates from Broome to Bondi.

Batter: Melt 1 tablespoon of butter or margarine. Add 1 cup of milk, 1 cup of self-raising flour, $^1/_2$ cup of caster sugar, $^1/_2$ cup of cocoa and 1 egg (optional). Mix ingredients into a batter and tip into a greased baking tray.

Sauce: Combine $1^1/_2$ cups of boiling water, $^1/_2$ cup of tightly packed brown sugar, $^1/_2$ cup of cocoa and a dash of vanilla, rum or brandy (optional).

Pour sauce over batter and bake for 20–30 minutes in a warm to hot oven (180–210ºC or 350–450ºF).

Cooking tips

➪ Entertain your housemates – do a *Two Fat Ladies* version of a cooking show (use your hands as mixers).

➪ If your housemate grunts in lieu of saying 'thank you for cooking a delicious dinner' or, more rudely, complains, simply insert three tablespoons of chilli into their next meal.

➪ If your housemate interferes with your cooking, chop the vegies in a frenzy ... with the meat cleaver.

➪ Order in pizza.

We all had similar skills levels as far as cooking goes. You can't be a gourmet cook in a six-person house but we all had our specialty dish. I cooked creamy vindaloo chicken — I used to make it from scratch and everyone loved it. But I cooked it for the girls I'm living with now when we first moved in and they didn't comment on it, there was just this silence. I was really hurt. I'm not cooking it for them again.

— Marianne

I've eaten really well in share-houses, lots of good recipes, but the only thing is it's nerve-racking, having to come up with something good for everyone else.

— Rebecca

Chapter 12

Meltdown

things can get really ugly in a share-house, but it's really only when someone gets kicked out or leaves that you discover how murky the tenancy legislation for share-houses can be. Unfortunately, most disputes between co-tenant housemates are not covered by tenancy legislation, so arguments over bond money, rent arrears, how much notice to give if you are leaving and other issues become a matter of negotiation, arm wrestling, nagging or blackmail.

The information provided here is intended as a guide only and not as a substitute for legal advice. Not only is the law different across the states and territories, but it is also complex, and the particulars of your situation will need to be taken into account. So make sure you get advice from a tenancy or legal service.

1. THE SHARE-HOUSE MELTDOWN

Share houses don't always melt down, but when do there will be some unmistakable signs that the house has lost that loving feeling.

KEY INDICATORS OF A HOUSE THAT'S REACHED ITS USE—BY DATE

⇨ No one joins you on the couch to watch the TV any more.

⇨ You can't recognise any of the fridge contents.

⇨ You are fantasising about whipping your housemate with the tea towels he hasn't washed.

⇨ Rude notes and sign language (particularly one-fingered signs) have replaced verbal communication.

⇨ You never see your housemates any more, in fact their rooms are empty.

Be prepared for the share-house meltdown. There's a total communication breakdown. People barricade themselves into bedrooms. Someone sets fire to the couch. Things start to go missing. There are bloody battles over who owns tea strainers and cheese graters.

Be prepared for the Runner. When the conflict has spun out of control, it's common for one housemate, or all, to disappear without paying bills or rent. In a meltdown situation, it can be wise to identify an item each of your housemates that you could hold hostage should they run off without paying the bills. Remove or hide your favourite things from the house. Get an ISD and STD bar on the phone *now*, to prevent someone making huge phone calls and never paying the bill.

If you suspect a housemate will disappear before the date they are supposed to move out, ask them to pay some bills in advance. Base your calculation on the average electricity, gas or water use per day (usually this is shown on the bill), and estimate how much they will owe up to the time when they are supposed to be leaving. That way, if they just disappear at least you've got some money out of them. It also saves you from having to discuss bills after the tenancy has ended.

2. TAKE CARE OUT THERE

You have the right to feel safe in your own home, and you should never be subjected to violence, sexual harassment, intimidation or threats by a housemate. You can call the police if you are afraid for your safety. If your housemate has turned sleazy or if you are feeling unsafe for other reasons you can get some free advice from your community legal service.

If you have been threatened or assaulted by a housemate, you may be able to apply for a restraining order to help protect you from further abuse (the legislation is different in each state and territory). The order is made by a court, and can include conditions that say that your housemate is not allowed to assault, threaten or harass you again, or is not allowed to come near you. If they break the conditions of the order they can be charged.

Restraining order

I'm living in this house in Croydon at the moment with two other guys. One of the guys is really bad. There's room for three cars to park in the driveway, and we usually have this order of how we park our cars. Then this one day I parked where he normally parks, and so he had to park behind me. He comes in and asks me to shift my car. I just said no, I'm not shifting. Then he gets really aggro and says, 'Well I'm going to park you in.' So he goes and parks across the driveway, so I can't get out. I needed to get to work. So I rang the cops and they came and gave him this parking ticket. When he got home he was just wild, he's like, 'I'll fucking kill you.'

The next day I come home and there's all this writing around the walls in the lounge that says, 'You're dead.' I went to the police and ended up taking out a restraining order. He was wild. The order says he can't assault or threaten me. We don't speak to each other now. He spends all his time in his bedroom with his TV. I'm basically the only person who uses the lounge room. The place is filthy. I clean my area, but no one else cleans. Too bad I couldn't have got the restraining order to say he had to clean the house.

— Dave

3. DRUG BUSTS

If there's a police raid in which your housemate's lost stash of cocaine is rediscovered down the side of couch, there is a possibility that you could get charged. This will depend on whether your housemate owns up, and on the police's perspective at the scene. Also, the drug laws differ throughout Australia. The information provided here is a general guide only – make sure you get information on what applies in your state or territory.

The severity of the offence generally depends upon the quantity of drugs found and whether the offence is deemed 'use', 'possession', 'cultivation', 'supply' or 'trafficking'. With a common or garden variety drug bust, police will need a warrant before they can search your premises. However, the police may enter your home without a warrant in certain circumstances for example, if you agree to them coming in or if they have reasonable grounds to believe that a serious offence is being or has been committed and entry is necessary to make an arrest.

You could be charged with possession if the drug is physically in your control (for example, if it is in your house). If you are living with a dealer there is a chance that you could get charged not only for possession, but also for assisting in supply/trafficking (for example, if you are shown to have knowingly made arrangements for someone else to sell or buy by phone).

There are a lot of myths about who can get done for what. So rather than finding out the hard way, contact your community legal centre who can advise you on the law in your state or territory.

4. YOUR STUFF

There are always going to be some items up for dispute when you move out. If you both swear that the frilly tablecloth is yours, you could flip a coin or compromise and have one person pay half the cost of the item. A dodgy housemate may think to take advantage of the fact that in the move you won't have noticed a few missing CDs. If you think there is a chance that your soon-to-be ex-housemate is not 100% honest then label your most important possessions and check their room before you finally depart.

5. ESCAPING YOUR SHARE-HOUSE AND GETTING YOUR BOND BACK

What you can and can't do in terms of leaving a tenancy depends whether you are a co-tenant, a head tenant, a sub-tenant, or a lodger/boarder, and the laws in your state or territory, so get information first from a tenancy or legal service.

If you all decide to leave the property, your legal responsibilities are set out in the residential tenancy legislation, including the amount of notice you have to give the landlord and the process of getting your bond back. The following information relates to situations where you want to leave but the others want to stay.

If you are a co-tenant: In most states there is no set period of notice that you legally have to give your co-tenants, but in terms of what is reasonable (rather than legal), a common practice in share-houses is that you give at least a month's notice. If you haven't already, make an agreement on how much notice is acceptable.

Before you move, contact the tenancy advice service in your state or territory and find out how to reduce your legal liability for the tenancy. While your name is still on the lease, you can be held legally liable for the rent and the condition of the property, even after you have moved out.

One way to end your legal responsibility for the tenancy is to ask your former co-tenants and your landlord to end the current tenancy agreement and enter into a new agreement. This way the landlord can inspect the condition of the property, so you will only be responsible for any damage up to the time you leave.

If this is not possible you may be able to assign or transfer your interest in the tenancy agreement to the remaining tenants, or to a new tenant if one moves in to replace you. This may reduce your legal liability for the property after you leave. You need the landlord's permission for this, but a landlord cannot unreasonably refuse to consent to the assignment of the tenancy. Make sure you confirm any agreement in writing. The process of assignment can be confusing, so it is really important to get advice from a tenancy advice service before you leave.

The remaining co-tenants, or the new tenant who moves in, should pay you out your share of the bond, and you should provide them with a full receipt. You should also notify the authority that is responsible for holding tenancy bonds (in states or territories where this exists) and make arrangements with them to transfer your bond to the new tenant.

Remember also to take your name off any bills. Contact the services you use to find out the process (there may be reconnection fees involved for your former housemates).

If you are the head tenant: If you decide to leave a property that you have been sub-letting, the sub-tenant would effectively have to leave too. In this case, you have to give the landlord the required period of notice in writing to end the tenancy agreement (the amount of notice required varies, depending on the kind of tenancy agreement you have). A sub-tenant who does not want to leave could try to negotiate a new tenancy agreement with the landlord.

If you are a sub-tenant: Legally you have to give the same amount of written notice to the head tenant as you would if you were giving notice to a landlord. The amount of notice depends on the kind of sub-tenancy agreement you have with the head tenant, and the laws in your state or territory. Alternatively, you may be able to come to some agreement with the head tenant on how much notice you should give. If there are any problems with the return of your bond, the dispute can usually be heard by the tribunal or court that deals with residential tenancies in your state or territory. Contact a tenancy advice or legal service.

If you are a boarder or lodger: If you are a boarder or a lodger you are generally not covered by the residential tenancy legislation. You are required to give 'reasonable notice' to leave (though people tend to have different ideas about what is reasonable). Disputes over rent owing or getting your bond back can be tricky for boarders or lodgers. If there is a dispute, you may be able to take the head tenant or owner to a local or magistrate's court to try to recover your money as a debt, but this can be costly.

6. MY HOUSEMATE'S DONE A RUNNER

This kind of thing often happens when there's serious conflict and some vindictive bastard wants to get you back for something. Other times the person is just desperate or irresponsible. Still, it can be a bloody nightmare.

If you are co-tenants: Unfortunately you can't claim that you are not responsible for housemates' share of rent.

Under a co-tenancy agreement, you are all liable, individually and jointly, for the rent. If one of your housemates has disappeared, you can be held liable for all the rent. If it is not paid in full, the landlord can institute proceedings to terminate the tenancy agreement.

You can try explaining the situation to the landlord and ask that they reduce the rent until you can get someone new in, but they are under no legal obligation to do this. You could try to track your ex-housemate down and demand that they pay you the money, or you could take them to a local or magistrate's court for compensation for the debt. You may also be able to claim compensation if they haven't paid bills, but this can be difficult and expensive.

If they've paid bond money, you may be able to keep it. The tenancy advice service in your state/territory can advise you on the process for getting the bond back in this situation.

If you are the head tenant and it's the sub-tenant who did a runner, you can apply to the residential tenancy tribunal or authority (just as your landlord could take action against you in the tribunal if you just left the property with rent owing). However, you are still responsible for their share of the rent in the meantime.

If you are the sub-tenant and it's the head tenant who has disappeared, then it's kind of a weird situation, because it's the head tenant whose name is on the lease. As a sub-tenant, you usually won't have had a direct or legal relationship with the landlord. Let the landlord know what happened in writing. Maybe they will let you stay on and sign a new lease agreement. Contact your tenancy advice service for more information.

7. MY HOUSEMATE'S DAMAGED THE PROPERTY

If one housemate (who is a co-tenant) causes damage and it is not fixed when the tenancy agreement ends, the money to cover the costs of repairs will probably come out of all of your bond money (not just from the bond of that housemate). And this may affect the rental reputation of all of you.

Hopefully you can agree with the housemate that they will cover any costs of damages, including repaying you if the landlord keeps the bond. Unfortunately, in most states and territories, the authority or tribunal that deals with residential tenancy legislation cannot hear disputes between co-tenants (there are exceptions – in Queensland, for example, disputes over bond between co-tenants can be taken to the Small Claims Tribunal). Often the only legal avenue you have is to take action against your housemate in a local or magistrate's court to recover the money, which is often time-consuming and expensive.

If you are the head tenant, you can apply to the tenancy tribunal (or similar authority) just as a landlord could, if you want to claim money for repairs from a sub-tenant's bond.

8. KICKING SOMEONE OUT

Attempting to kick someone out is a delicate and difficult business. Hopefully you all accept that the situation isn't working and the person will agree to go.

Whether you can legally force someone to leave depends on your tenancy status.

As the head tenant you can legally ask a sub-tenant to leave, but you have to follow the same procedure a landlord would have to follow. This means that legally you have to give the sub-tenant a set period of notice in writing. The amount of notice depends on the legislation in your state or territory and on why you are asking them to leave. There have been cases where a sub-tenant has taken the head tenant to the tribunal for not giving the correct notice to leave.

Why it's important to know your responsibilities: a case example

A tenant who rented a house got a new tenant in. The new tenant paid rent and bond to her, so she effectively became the head tenant and the new person was the sub-tenant. Conflict occurred between the two and the head tenant forcibly removed the sub-tenant and threw the sub-tenant's possessions out on the footpath. The tribunal in New South Wales found that the head tenant had failed to give proper notice to the sub-tenant and therefore had breached the Residential Tenancies Act 1997.

— Goddard, Kessel & Associates and Stamatellis, 1998:33

As the sub-tenant you can't legally ask the head tenant to leave. You can take action under the residential tenancies legislation if they have breached any of their legal obligations in relation to you (for example, if they have not arranged for the repairs you requested to be done). But a tribunal or similar authority can only order the head tenant to remedy the breach, not to move out.

Co-tenants do not generally have the legal right to kick each other out, so asking someone to leave becomes a matter of negotiation. It's best to talk to the person face to face (assuming there have been no threats or violence). Usually someone gets asked to leave if all the other housemates agree that things aren't working. It could be due to incompatibility, or perhaps the person has not been pulling their weight or sticking to agreements. Whatever the reason, it can be quite humiliating to be asked to leave. If the situation is not likely to change, go with the 'it's unfortunate, but things are not working, we are not compatible' approach. The amount of notice you give is something to negotiate. In most situations, it's fair to give plenty of notice. You might also agree that if they find a place more quickly, they will be refunded any rent that they have paid in advance.

In some situations, you may feel justified in giving your housemate very little notice to leave, for instance if a person has done something to cause serious harm to other housemates.

What if they refuse to go?

Confronted by a majority of people who don't want you there, most people will just pack up and get out as soon as possible. However, a housemate with fairly thick skin or a sense of self-righteousness may refuse to go. If you are in a two-person household and you ask the other person to leave, you should probably be prepared for, 'I'm not going anywhere. If you don't like it here, why don't you leave?'

Often if the person digs in their heels and refuses to go, it becomes a matter of endurance — who can withstand the tension the longest. Dispute resolution or mediation can help co-tenants negotiate through these problems. But all parties have to be prepared to negotiate. Contact your local tenancy advice service or community legal centre to find out what services are available.

But because life is not fair, no matter how justified you feel, you may have to just cut your losses and go yourself.

Meltdowns

It was the end of the uni year and my housemates were both trying to get their assignments finished. I was exhausted from working a lot of overtime. I would come home at the end of the day and there would be this real atmosphere in the house. The lease was about to finish so we decided to move out. One housemate, Julie, took off for Canberra and only showed up on the last day. I was stressed with the cleaning. But my other housemate, Rosalba, went completely spare. When Julie finally arrived, Rosalba started screaming, 'Where the hell have you been?' But Julie could hold her ground and was kind of ignoring Rosalba. Rosalba finally just sort of sank to the floor, crying. I started yelling at Julie, and we were standing really close and she was yelling back, going 'na na na na'. I've got no idea what she was saying. She was boiling and I was boiling, and then I hit her. She was absolutely horrified, she ran out the back. A friend of mine who was also there said something like, 'Steady on, steady on, there's no need for that.' Rosalba was still collapsed on the floor. Her teenage niece, who had been staying over, had witnessed the whole thing. She goes, 'Wow, this is a great holiday.'

— Sandra

The perfect housemate (not)

I thought I'd found the perfect housemate. Phoebe was so nice – she was really good at listening to my work problems and she'd cook these great meals. We became really close. About six months after she moved in she got this fantastic job writing for a national newspaper. I was totally amazed because she'd said she'd just finished her journalism degree and didn't have any work experience as far as I knew. How could she land a job like that? Admittedly I was jealous because I'd been working as a journalist in crappy jobs for years, but I was happy for her.

One weekend she was out and my computer crashed, so I decided to use hers to type a letter to the bank. As I was opening files, I noticed a file for the letter Phoebe had sent to apply for the newspaper job she now had. When I opened it, I couldn't believe it. The letter basically described my work history. Her c.v. was identical to mine, even my uni results. The only difference was that my name was replaced by hers and the referees were different. How could she do this to me? She'd used my work to get the job.

When I confronted her she went totally white. She admitted what she'd done, but she cried so much for so long I started feeling sorry for her. We agreed that it would be best for her to move out. But the next day when I came home from work, she was gone, disappeared, left no money for bills, nothing. I rang where she worked and she hadn't shown up – they didn't know where she was.

Two weeks later I got my credit card statement and there were all these things I hadn't paid for on it, including motel accommodation and an airfare to Sydney. I searched my room for my credit card, but it was gone. I felt so horrible reporting her, it was like I was in a nightmare. I still couldn't believe what she'd done to me. They never tracked her down. Since then I've been incredibly cautious about housemates.

– Raewyn

We asked one of our housemates to leave. He'd just been a total arsehole. He refused to leave so we decided to try to freeze him out. You'd walk past each other in the hallway and press yourself against the wall to be as far away from each other as you could. We all got locks on our doors. There were bags of food in the fridge with 'keep off' signs on them. We kept toilet paper in our rooms, so he'd have to get his own or suffer. Everyone moved their possessions to their bedrooms, so they were really crowded with kitchen appliances, chairs, etc., and there was hardly any furniture in the rest of the house. We used a mobile phone because we couldn't trust him not to wipe any messages off the answering machine. This went on for two months. We weren't getting anywhere. We rang the tenants' union and they suggested we go to a dispute resolution service. For some reason he agreed to come along. The mediation did nothing really but it was good to have other people there

> *and to say what you thought. Then about two weeks later,*
> *he just did a runner. Trashed things in the kitchen, smashed*
> *stuff, left owing rent and bills. By this stage, we didn't want*
> *the house any more anyway, so we left too. Too many bad*
> *memories.*
>
> — Paul

A FEW FINAL WORDS

When you've experienced a few share-house meltdowns, you start to operate with low expectations. You won't expect much of your housemates; in fact, if someone moves out without stealing your CDs and owing less than $200 you feel like you're doing well. You don't expect much of the house; in fact you are pleasantly surprised if you survive there for a year without being killed by falling debris. You'll expect nothing of real estate agents and are never surprised.

Although some people out in share-house land are wolves in sheeps' clothing, not all of them are. Remember, in a share-house you see people at their worst. You see them when they crawl through the door drunk with one eyebrow shaved off at 5 a.m. You see them with bed hair in the morning or grumpy and depressed at the end of a working day. You get to know their bad habits, drug habits, strange friends and personal hygiene problems. And they get to know yours.

While it's impossible always to predict weirdness and to avoid arguments, there are ways of reducing the likelihood of problems and conflict, as this guide has tried to demonstrate. Your most important prevention strategies are to screen potential housemates carefully and to have clear agreements at the start.

Sharing a house can be a good experience if you are living with people you get along with and who are reliable and thoughtful. There are lots of bad housemates out there, but they do make you more appreciative of the good ones.

Take it from the US roommate's handbook (*52 Ways To Get Along With Your College Roommate*) which offers these comforting thoughts: 'Recognise that even though you are no longer roommates sharing a room, house or apartment, you will continue to be two people sharing the same planet. As such, you are still in relationship – however distant – and will be all your lives.'

Scary, isn't it?

Useful contacts

The following services can provide advice about residential tenancy matters, including information about your tenancy status.

Tenancy advice services

Tenancy advice services help tenants with disputes with landlords and sub-tenants in disputes with head tenants. However, they may not be able to assist with disputes between co-tenants or to advise head tenants in matters relating to sub-tenants or boarding. In some states and territories, tenancy advice lines operate limited hours, so don't leave it till last thing Friday afternoon to ring them.

Dispute resolution or mediation services

Mediation or dispute resolution services can help you to negotiate your share-house dispute in a co-operative way (usually at no cost). You can contact these services for advice on resolving a dispute or to arrange for you and your housemates to meet with a professional mediator. A mediator will not take sides in the dispute, but can help you to negotiate fairly and come to an agreement. A tenancy advice service or community legal centre can refer you to the appropriate service in your state or territory, or look them up in the government section of your telephone book under *Complaints and disputes.*

Government departments – consumer affairs or fair trading

Each state and territory has a government department responsible for fair trading and consumer affairs. The tenancy section of these departments can provide advice on residential tenancy matters and on lodging and boarding situations. They should be listed in the government section of your telephone directory.

Share-house matching agencies

In most states and territories private agencies can assist with finding share accommodation and housemates (fees apply). These agencies can match you up with a house or a housemate that suits your requirements. Most advertise in the share-accommodation section of newspapers and in specialist publications such as the gay and lesbian press. Many also provide their services via the internet – search with words such as flatmate, share accommodation, share-house, flat sharing, gay share, etc.

Community legal centres

Community legal centres provide free legal advice on tenancy matters, lodging and boarding and legal aspects of share-house disputes. The telephone numbers below are for the secretariat in each state or territory. Call them and ask to be referred to your local legal centre.

Australian Capital Territory

Tenant Advice Service	Ph. 02 6247 2011
ACT Association of Community Legal Centres	Ph. 02 6247 2177

New South Wales

Tenants Union of NSW	Ph. 02 9251 6590
NSW Community Legal Centre Secretariat	Ph. 02 9318 2355

Northern Territory

Darwin Community Legal Centre Inc.	Ph. 08 8982 1111

Queensland

Tenants Union Queensland	Ph. 07 3257 1108
North Qld	Ph. 07 4031 3194
Caxton Legal Centre	Ph. 07 3254 1811

South Australia

Office of Consumer & Business Affairs	
Tenancies branch	Ph. 08 8204 9544
Norwood Community Legal Centre	Ph. 08 8362 1199

Tasmania

Tenants Union Tasmania	
Hobart	Ph. 03 6223 2641
Other areas	Ph. 1300 652 641
Tasmanian Association of Community	
Legal Centres	Ph. 03 6223 2500

Victoria

Tenants Union of Victoria	Ph. 03 9416 2577
Web site address	www.tuv.org.au
Victorian Federation of Community Legal Centres	Ph. 03 9602 4949

Western Australia

Tenants Advice Service	Ph. 1800 621 888 or
	08 9221 0088
Web site address	www.taswa.org.au
WA Federation of Community Legal Centres	Ph. 08 9221 9322

References

Australian Bureau of Statistics (1999), *Labour Force Status and Other Characteristics of Families*, Catalogue Number 6224.0, Canberra.

Australian Bureau of Statistics (1996), *1996 Census of Population and Housing Australia*, Canberra.

Baum, Frances (1986), 'Shared Housing: Making Alternative Lifestyles Work', *Australian Journal of Social Issues*, Vol. 21, no. 3, pp. 197–212.

Bureau of Immigration and Population Research (1994), *The Social Characteristics of Immigrants in Australia*, Australian Government Publishing Service, Canberra.

Jane Goddard, Kessels and Associates and Stamatia Stamatellis (1998), *The Fair Share: reform of residential tenancies law in NSW as it relates to share housing*, Tenants Union of NSW.